This is Stephen Morris' second novel. His first, *Memoir, A Novel by Stella Kelly*, was published by Austin Macauley in 2019.

Stephen Morris

THE WINTER ARCHIVIST

AUSTIN MACAULEY PUBLISHERS™
LONDON • CAMBRIDGE • NEW YORK • SHARJAH

Copyright © Stephen Morris (2021)

The right of Stephen Morris to be identified as author of this work has been asserted by the author in accordance with section 77 and 78 of the Copyright, Designs and Patents Act 1988.

All rights reserved. No part of this publication may be reproduced, stored in a retrieval system, or transmitted in any form or by any means, electronic, mechanical, photocopying, recording, or otherwise, without the prior permission of the publishers.

Any person who commits any unauthorised act in relation to this publication may be liable to criminal prosecution and civil claims for damages.

This is a work of fiction. Names, characters, businesses, places, events, locales, and incidents are either the products of the author's imagination or used in a fictitious manner. Any resemblance to actual persons, living or dead, or actual events is purely coincidental.

A CIP catalogue record for this title is available from the British Library.

ISBN 9781398421097 (Paperback)
ISBN 9781398421103 (ePub e-book)

www.austinmacauley.com

First Published (2021)
Austin Macauley Publishers Ltd
25 Canada Square
Canary Wharf
London
E14 5LQ

# Part One

Despite her reluctance even to come to the flat, let alone enter it, the key slid into the lock without resistance. It was well used and as Catherine turned it, she gently pushed to open the front door. She felt the door continue to resist and looking below the Yale lock she saw another keyhole further down the door. She only had one key and almost gave up at this point. It had after all taken her some time to summon up, was it courage, nerve anyway to come here. When she arrived at the red brick mansion block in Bloomsbury not so far from the British Museum, she feared most the watchful eye of a concierge as she entered the building using the fob that came to her with the key. This building did not enjoy that luxury. Residents came and went without supervision except, she presumed, video. No concierge meant there was no one to ask how she could overcome the second lock. Now that there was an obstacle to her entry into the flat, Ben's flat, she became more determined to get in. It was the push she needed to complete what she had come to describe as an obligation to her friend, acquaintance really. Puzzled by the absence of a second key to open the lower lock, it occurred to her to try the same key in that lock as well. Like the first lock the key slid in smoothly and turned without any difficulty. The door opened and she entered Ben's flat.

She was keen to close the door behind her. She felt like a thief. She had never imagined herself breaking and entering, and in truth she hadn't broken and entered this time. Still this was not violence against someone else's privacy or person. That was not possible as Ben was dead. He lived alone at least as far as she knew. Then she was not so sure she knew all that much about this man she had met only so recently and whose so sudden death had brought her over his threshold.

When Ben had died it was unexpected. She thought it would have been as unexpected for him as it was for her. He had been marginally overweight and drank wine at their occasional lunches. Yet he seemed without vices or ailments. She had only heard that he had died after the solicitor contacted her. Heart failure. He had described the circumstances. Ben had felt ill returning from a trip to the Continent. He had gone to the GP the following day. An ambulance had been called and twenty-four hours after admission he had died.

On her fourth visit, she was sure it was her fourth, she felt more confident in the flat. Thief-like to begin with, she had looked through things, carefully replacing them so that Ben would not know she had disturbed them. Now, she accepted that this was senseless. It felt to her like sacrilege and she wondered why she continued to pry at Ben's belongings – of which there were not so many.

Having never been burgled herself, she was unsure what the worst part of the experience was for the burgled. Another potter she had known at college left London when her flat was burgled and moved to Devon where she lived very unhappily for a few years. That seemed to Catherine overdone. She chastised herself for such a judgement. If that seemed the right thing for her friend to do, so be it. They had not been close and lost touch, so perhaps she had settled eventually in her Devon life.

She had brought some shopping. The first couple of times she hadn't thought it right to help herself to drinks or food. Now she argued the legacy was itself an invitation from Ben to have a drink. She put the milk in the fridge. She had emptied it of its contents on her first visit but hadn't switched it off. Now it was useful as a fridge; carrying on functioning regardless of the death of its owner. Fridges didn't die, they broke and eventually became irreparable. In the kitchen of his small flat, she looked at the washing machine, the dishwasher with suspicion. Her finger prints were beginning to appear everywhere. Did they displace Ben's or were they superimposed? If she were done for burglary would the police be able to use them as evidence of her breaking and entering? Still, she consoled herself, she hadn't broken, only entered.

When an apparently healthy man in his sixties, whom you met at your Italian class, asks you, over a coffee, to be the executor of his will, you do what Catherine had done. You say you'll think about it. A holding manoeuvre she often deployed because she did need to think about it. Ben said of course, he understood, and had wanted to explain why he was asking her. After all they had only known each other for a short time. Meeting first over coffee to practise speaking Italian. Then subsequently, as they had found some pleasure in the chance to talk about politics, art, books – those kinds of things – arranged to visit exhibitions and see films. They both remained reserved, tight lipped, about that area of personal intimacy. He spoke about his childhood and his parents. Listening, Catherine heard a barrier drop on anyone later in his life who might have engendered love. Ben spoke about his role as archivist at the Winter Institute, and it was with intensity, but the individuals were holders of office, people of virtue and vision, colleagues, superiors, leaders. If they had souls, they failed to express them in the day to day flesh of love and passion.

She had bought a pint of milk. She resented that it cost so much more to buy small amounts. She made herself coffee, instant, that she had also bought. Ben had some ground coffee in a tin he kept in the fridge which she had thrown away on the first day of her fridge clear out. Then she had stopped. Her brain told her you are supposed to empty out a dead person's flat. Dispose of the possessions sensitively. Give objects of value to relations or friends who might find them sentimental. Donate books and clothes to charity shops. Get rid of things quickly that might go off or were of little or no value. By her second visit she had changed her mind. She didn't want to rush.

Of course, the most pressing thing had been the dog. It was a small cross breed terrier kind of dog. She did not like and was slightly allergic to dogs and cats. She was especially critical of Ben for having a dog as he lived in a small flat in central London. He rebuffed that criticism roundly. The dog had a wonderful life. Walks in Russell Square and on occasion out to Hampstead on the bus. Pampered, the dog had all the pleasure of being devoted and loyal to its fond master. It was a great life. For the dog's good fortune, he was staying in his holiday kennel where Ben had put him during his trip. As the dog was a regular, he stayed on amongst the confusion of Ben's death. When Catherine tracked the dog down, the owner of the kennels was more distressed than she had been at the news of Ben's death. He hadn't known how to break it to the dog. This Catherine found ridiculous and then as ever self-censured for being so judgemental. People love dogs, and this man also appeared very fond of Ben. He also wanted to know what she wanted to do about the dog. He needed a home.

It would be an undue burden if her obligations as executor extended to taking in the dog. The dog would not be happy. She would not be happy. She spoke to the kennel owner about her dilemma, which he immediately solved. There was a dog homing service run by one of his friends, a charity. He spoke lovingly of the importance that the dog's grief be enabled by finding new owners who could not replace Ben, but who could signal a new start. No more walks in the square listening to the traffic, but the joy perhaps of the country or of being with a family with children. So, the dog was homed and Ben's dog apparatus donated to the kennels – much appreciated – along with a substantial payment for additional costs and a conscience easing donation to the dog homing charity. It surprised Catherine how much of her time this was all taking.

The flat was small on the Bloomsbury side of King's Cross. Sitting in the living room she surveyed once again the contents. Small bathroom, bit old fashioned with a ropey shower. Kitchen too small to cook in properly, although Ben had cooked his own food. Bedroom with built in wardrobe and chest of drawers. From the living room, Catherine could see into all the rooms plus the tiny hallway mainly occupied by a coat stand. Ben's coats were still there. She would need to do something about his clothes. Charity shop – did they collect? She did feel overwhelmed; overwhelmed in so many ways. There was the practical reality of sorting out the flat so abruptly vacated but also on her mind what was she supposed to do next. Ben had left no instructions. She had not been able to conceal her astonishment when Ben's solicitor had told her that not only was she the executor of Ben's will, but also his sole inheritor. He had left the lot to her. She asked the solicitor to repeat that, so he did and also asked, which he shouldn't have done, whether she knew he was leaving everything to her. She had said, perplexedly, that she would need to think about it. She sat with her cup of coffee, a thief in Ben's flat, still thinking about it.

The next time they met after Ben asked Catherine to be his executor she said she didn't mind if that would be helpful for him. He said she could get his solicitor to do all the work, she would just need to sign the papers. He was grateful and bought her a second cappuccino. Now, she reflected, if she had asked him, or allowed him to explain his reasons, would he have mentioned that his will left everything to her. Why was that? They really were acquaintances, friends of a sort, yes, but nothing beyond the chance to chat and confer about the world as it is and as it might be, might have been.

She came again the next day. She had not meant to visit so often. She brought one of her pots from the studio in Crouch End where she lived. The 91 bus was almost door to door, she argued. There was so much to do, so much to sort out. She had a routine now. Her sixth visit? First she put the shopping she had bought on the way into the fridge. If she reflected, she would have known that the perishable lunch things suggested a more regular routine of visiting than she yet admitted to herself. Cheese, ham, some olives, two pints of milk this time and some salad things. She also brought cottage cheese and tins of sweetcorn and tuna. It turned out to be more than she had realised as she unpacked her bag. She wanted to have choices for her lunches. Next she made her instant coffee and then went into the living room to sit. She had placed the pot, it was a squat, plainly glazed vase, on the coffee table where she now rested her mug. It was like a job. Still she did not yet know the task or that she would become a regular commuter on the 91 bus.

They did not visit each other's homes. She remembered Ben's appearance at the intermediate Italian class she had been attending on and off for a number of years. He was shy and hesitant with a natural anxiety as a newcomer to an established class of adult learners who knew each other's abilities. The teacher invited each of them to introduce themselves and say a little of what they had been doing in the holidays. Everyone struggled through it, including Ben, and there was the usual sense of relief that no one was that bad and no one was especially good. In the second week, they were partnered as is the way of these things and Catherine learned more about him. He lived in London. He had worked abroad in France for many years. He had visited Venice quite frequently as part of his work.

The suggestion for a conversation group had been made by the teacher half way through the term. Emails were shared and there was an enthusiasm that did not carry through to the first gathering. Only the two of them turned up at the coffee bar designated for the get together near the college. They had dutifully spoken a stilted Italian until, at Ben's suggestion, they had reverted to English so that they could at least, as he put it, get to know each other a little better. That way their Italian conversations might become more than where they lived, what they did, what they liked. Or not, he had joked.

Catherine was relieved to move to English. She was as interested in him as he appeared to be in her. Few friends, he explained, as he was something of a loner which he put down to being an only child growing up in quite a poor home that his parents helped him escape by getting to university. However, his education only estranged him from the children he had grown up with. Practically their lives moved far apart, and he lost touch with them only keeping links with his mum and dad. Catherine was persuaded that this was truthful. That mattered to her, people who did not embellish or reinvent themselves. On the strength of his apparent honesty, she explained her own circumstances. She was a potter by training and inclination. As that made little money, she also worked stints as a graphic artist and also taught at her local college to supplement her income. They didn't need to ask each other anything else. That was enough to be going on with, more would test their reliability and be too fast. There was plenty of time to get to know each other, although, as it turned out, not enough.

They met at the National Gallery. He told her (in Italian) he had a dog. She asked him whereabouts in London he lived and he told her Bloomsbury. The Italian conversations on where you live never having got beyond London, central London. They had the discussion (started in Italian and ending in English) about owning a dog in a flat in central London. In turn they each took the other to their favourite paintings. She took him to the Bellinis and he took her to the Vermeers. They both thought that was a good start. Really she wanted to choose Van Gogh's sunflowers or Monet's lilies, but she was hesitant and embarrassed at the obviousness of her choices. It was a small dissimulation. She hoped he wouldn't mind.

She drank the coffee. By thinking back over what he had said, where they had met, what they had done, she hoped to conjure a picture of this now dead man that would help her understand what she was doing here and why he had left her everything. Once she had accepted the request to be his executor he never explained why he had asked her and she did not think to ask. She noticed on his desk the little ochre bowl she had potted and given him at Christmas. That was nearly a year ago now. She had known him over a year then. She had only just now noticed it on her sixth visit. There was something not quite right. She was in some delayed shock, at any rate not thinking right. As a result, the desk came into focus and she got up and went over to look at it more closely. She put down her coffee on it and pulled open the middle drawer. It was mahogany and old fashioned, an antique even. There was an area for writing where the chair went and then on the right-hand side a column of three other drawers. The drawer she had pulled out was underneath the writing area. In it were neat piles of papers – some financial statements, a barely used cheque book. In the other three drawers were various sets of index cards. She picked some up, careful that they remained in the same order. Ben had written notes on each one. It would take time to understand all of this.

She still needed to sort out his clothes. There were bin liners already in the flat. She would use these and according to the website the British Heart Foundation would be happy to collect them. Heart failure made this appealing to her. It was an unenjoyable task in every way. It surprised her when she had finished and there were only four bags of clothes. That was all he had needed. He had one suit, three pairs of shoes and a pair of boots. Slippers and sandals. He hadn't needed much to get through. Inevitably sad, she felt grief slip through her hair and fingers like a shower of dust leaving a partial print. She washed her hands before making a ham and cheese salad. She added some of the sweetcorn. The bags of clothes were by the front door. She remembered the call from the solicitor.

She never answered her phone these days. Most people contacted her electronically. An actual phone call usually meant some recorded message offering her a funeral plan. If it was important, then the caller could leave a message. It was also inconvenient when she was working with her hands covered in clay or decorating one of her pots before taking them to the kiln at the local community college. She barely noticed the phone ringing. Later she remembered that it had rung and looked up the number – withheld. She listened to the messages. It was Ben's solicitor (she hadn't known, but she later worked this out) asking her to call him as he understood she was the executor of Ben's will. So she did and that is how she discovered he had died unexpectedly and quickly of heart failure.

The solicitor's office was in Holborn. The meeting had been quick. As usual, the solicitor was absurdly young. She had signed some papers. He explained what would happen next. It should all be tied up quite quickly as the will was very straightforward. She was the sole beneficiary. She asked him to repeat this. He did and made his enquiry whether she knew. There was a pause. Was he waiting for her to say or do something? Was there some formality she had missed out on? She said she would need to think about it. As they shook hands, he looked impatient – perplexed she wondered. She would need to come back to the office to sign papers once the matter was concluded. She looked at him, or, he had added, they could send the papers. She left.

Eating her cheese and ham salad, the pause she had experienced in the solicitor's office continued. She had paused her work, her usual routine and replaced them with these increasingly frequent visits to the home of an acquaintance she didn't really know. She had also paused on what to do about all this. Sorting out the clothes was one thing – practical, like emptying the fridge – but what about the flat? What about all the things like the index cards? Not only the index cards, but there were many files. Each neatly catalogued with a contents page. That was who Ben had been, an archivist.

She had met Alain at the crematorium where Ben's funeral was held. It was after the visit with the solicitor. Alain had introduced himself. There were only five people at the funeral. No sign of the solicitor. Alain knew who she was. Ben must have spoken to him about her. It was Alain, she realised, who had organised the funeral, not the solicitor as she had imagined since he had provided her with the details.

Alain had been the assistant archivist to Ben at the Winter Institute. It was Alain whom Ben had been visiting in Grenoble just before he died and it was Alain who had returned to London with him and been with him while he was dying in those few hours in a London hospital. Alain had stayed on in London. He understood how things were with the legacy and the will. There appeared no hard feeling or sense of being owed by Ben. The reverse, Alain remembered Ben with love and respect, speaking of him affectionately as not only a colleague but a great friend.

The funeral was brief and practical. The other three people – Catherine never found out who they were – left immediately. That was when Alain introduced himself, outside the crematorium and they struck up something of a friendship while he stayed on in his B&B in Willesden Green. She invited him to the flat when they first met at the crematorium, but he preferred they met in coffee shops. That is how Ben and he always met. When they met, Alain told her about the Winter Institute. Originally based in Grenoble, it had opened a second cultural centre in Venice and then moved its headquarters to the beautiful mountain village of Versur not far from Grenoble, where it retained a European cultural centre. Alain had always lived in Grenoble, unlike everyone else, unlike Ben, who lived in Versur. Versur, the home of the Winter Institute and the world famous English Speaking Theatre. Alain had joined the Institute after Ben. Ben had recruited him. By the time Alain had arrived, the Winter Institute and Versur had to all intents and purposes become one and the same. Herr Winter, the son of the original Herr Winter, the Swiss family that had established the Winter Institute, was in reality the patron of Versur. He would never admit it, but the mayor was always his nominee. Why not, as Versur benefited enormously from the wealth of the Institute. That is why they all lived there, in the rent free accommodation provided as part of the generous remuneration arrangements. They all left once they left the Institute, most, of course, because of age, because of retirement although the family had no strict policies on an appropriate retirement age. How could they, when the elder Herr Winter had continued for so long as the head – titular and real – until he had died aged 95.

Alain was helpful in filling in some of the gaps in her knowledge from her acquaintance with Ben. When Catherine met with Ben it was to visit somewhere he had suggested – an exhibition for example. The attempts to practise Italian fizzled out. Reaching Elephant and Castle from Crouch End was not the easiest journey for Catherine. She was intrigued nonetheless why Ben had chosen this destination. The area was definitely ugly, even by London's low standards. Ben met her outside the Bakerloo line tube entrance. He was very specific which was just as well since there were no clear meeting points, just loads of different bus stops. He smiled appreciatively at her no nonsense punctuality.

Today they would be taking a trip down his memory lane. He was apologetic.

"My childhood is all here."

He guided her through the Walworth Road and towards East Street. The shops sold mainly second hand goods. Lots of used technology. There was a pawn shop. The pub they passed was boarded up. There was a café offering all day breakfasts at a knock down price.

"All my life, this area's been on the brink of gentrification."

It had a long way to go, was how Catherine perceived it.

Across the road from East Street market – which was busy and more interesting – lay a road of terraced houses and Ben indicated the one in which he had grown up. Proud parents of an unusually clever little boy they were determined should have an education and make something of himself.

"And he did, he became the Winter Archivist."

How do you archive winter? Still, Catherine knew better than to ask. They continued walking past the market and towards Camberwell. Ben seemed ready to reminisce. Catherine thought of her own childhood home. No, she would not wish to take Ben or anyone there. For Ben this was a huge degree of an intimacy she knew made him feel deeply uncomfortable.

She told Alain about that particular excursion. It was sentimental but also touching. Alain recognised Ben's playfulness masking a real sense of feeling that rarely made it to the surface. Alain did not know the other funeral attenders. He seemed uninterested in them. In each subsequent coffee encounter, Catherine became more and more aware of Alain's grief. She was now a substitute for Ben, a place where he could attach his sadness. This was in no way demonstrative. It was just present as a continuous note to their conversations; conversations that were invariably about Ben. Yet Catherine felt no great grief for this man she had got to know more or less by chance quite recently relative to their own ages. They were both old, older than Alain. Alain was still at a stage when you went to work. Catherine wondered what he did now since he had left his post at the Winter Institute some time ago. She wondered how long he intended to stay at the B&B before returning to Grenoble.

Alain solved that by announcing when they next met that he was going to go back to Grenoble. He wanted Catherine to come and visit. He wanted to show her Versur. He suggested it would be better in the summer. Catherine agreed vaguely and made her own invitation in return. She really wanted Alain to come and have lunch or supper with her in Ben's flat before he went back to Grenoble. She could see immediately that this invitation was unexpected. Alain did not indicate it was unwelcome, he just was not prepared and so had not decided how to respond, except politely. Catherine found this partly cold, partly hard to read. She did not want to ascribe to Alain feelings of reluctance that may not have existed or even begin to speculate on the nature of his friendship with Ben. Ben, it was now surely apparent, was quite odd. Odder than Alain, she did not know, or herself really when she put her mind to exploring what she was doing in her seventies visiting almost daily the flat of a man she had barely known. A flat she now owned.

Catherine's studio was in a converted shed at the end of the short garden attached to the one bedroomed garden flat where she had lived now for more than thirty years. The only drawback to the studio, apart from being hard to heat in the winter, was the absence of space for a kiln. For firings, she relied on the community college kiln where she also taught. She taught to earn money and to maintain access to the kiln, but it was not something she enjoyed. Sometimes, when her studio became so cold in the winter months, she also potted at the college. In the deep cold, her clay became unworkable, water freezing to the touch. However, she disliked working in a public space. She craved privacy. Her other job, to keep the wolves from the door, was as a freelance graphic artist. Her work was in demand but she disliked almost everything about doing this. The absence of choice or creativity in the subject matter. For her, creativity was not about solving the problem of how to represent, but the action of representing. That was how she had learned to explain this to colleagues who took exception to her dislike of working as a graphic artist. She did not feel the need to think on about it further than that statement, a holding statement she avoided using as she avoided giving her opinion in any public forum. Which she also disliked about her work. As with the community college, she was exposed to working in a public space.

Now, however, it was a pre-Christmas cold snap and she needed to abandon the chilly studio where the bottled gas heater made her feel she was camping and take her work to the public space. She wished to believe there was no public gaze, that she imagined this, but as often was the case one of her students – they were all or had been her students by this time – was in the studio and keen to know what she was working on. Catherine had no way of explaining the multiple complications she was experiencing in her potting just then. After several years of being engulfed in a totally enjoyable experience of making thrown objects with applied figures she had now decided to change tack, but no alternative tack readily came up. She had experimented with slab in her own studio but didn't wish to continue with that here. Then there were the now frequent visits to Bloomsbury. These disrupted her rhythm; both the regularity of the hours she spent potting, but also the continuity of how she thought about her pots, the new phase she was about to embark on. Then there was Ben's death and now Alain. None of this she could discuss with her eager student, whose name she had forgotten and didn't like to be seen as rude by needing to ask.

Catherine asked in return – always ask a question when you don't want to answer what you have been asked had been a tactic she deployed for many years – what her student thought a middle aged Frenchman visiting from Grenoble to attend the funeral of an older, former colleague would like to have for dinner. Now that Alain had accepted her invitation and indicated that dinner would suit him better than lunch, Catherine faced the dilemma of what to cook. She did not think she was a bad cook. She might have become a bit eccentric, as she cooked exclusively for herself. If she had lunch or dinner with friends, it would be in a restaurant. She hadn't entertained, she found herself explaining to the slightly bemused student, for an indeterminate period of probably decades. Now, she couldn't imagine what had led her to invite Alain in the first place. That was not true but was a necessary lie to avoid the need to explain to this relative stranger the real reason. The real reason was that she wanted Alain to visit the flat. She needed an endorsement from him of Ben's work there; an expert opinion, so to speak.

Surprisingly to Catherine, the student – was it Susan, she dare not risk getting her name wrong, even ruder than asking her what it was – had a really good idea. She also introduced herself as Kate. How could Catherine possibly remember all her students' names. Catherine was warming to Kate, more interested in what she was working on than speaking about herself. Kate's idea, and she recognised the particular fear of an English woman cooking dinner for a Frenchman, was to go for Christmas dinner. With Christmas a few weeks away, there should be turkeys available and it was something unique and of the place so there could be no unfortunate comparisons with French cuisine. Brilliant, Catherine congratulated Kate. What was Kate working on, slab, interesting, but such small pieces.

Catherine, inspired by Kate, decided on roast turkey. She would skip the Christmas pudding and mince pies, neither of which she enjoyed as both were stodgy and coarsely spiced. She would buy some expensive baklava for afters with coffee, which she would not be able to drink as now it kept her up all night. She potted. Giving Kate the benefit of the doubt she worked on slab here in the community college. Kate had needed to go and the other two potters working there were strangers to Catherine. She made a medium sized, crude four sided oblong dish about four inches in height and width, just over six inches long. It would be good for the Brussel sprouts. She left it there in the drying room. It would be a gift for Alain, a Christmas present at the Christmas dinner. She thought of it as crude – deliberately so – he would describe it later to his friends as rustic and charming – a traditionally glazed serving dish.

Alain came to dinner at Ben's flat the day before he was scheduled to return to Grenoble and leave the Willesden B&B where he had stayed for over a month. In that month the flat had changed and not changed. There was certainly a lot more of Catherine apparent. In the kitchen there were fridge things and dry goods that meant she could have her lunch there and make drinks. In the living room a number of pots had arrived, mainly decorative, and also flowers in vases from her studio. The bathroom was now for her not for Ben. Ben's everyday things had been removed. His toiletries, food, clothes all binned or given away. What remained were his pictures, his books, ornaments and things like pens. Above all what remained were records – the index cards, the boxes containing folders and files of papers, the notebooks each written by Ben with detailed and annotated lists, paragraphs of writing some of which looked like transcripts of interviews, diaries. So many records, it was difficult to understand how Ben could need them. She had found a whole stash more in a deep store cupboard behind the hat stand in the tiny hallway.

She did not live there. She remained a visitor. There was enough of Ben for it to feel like his flat. There was enough of her to make her comfortable. What she did not know was what to do with it. The obvious thing to do would be to sell it, but she hesitated.

"This feels exactly like Ben's place in Versur" were Alain's first words when he had settled with a glass of red wine on the sofa in the living room. "Are you keeping it the same? Surely you need to sell it now Ben is gone. Isn't it time to move on?"

Alain liked to ask her questions and she replied in her usual way to ask him what he thought she should do.

"I don't know," he replied. "It is morbid to keep it as a shrine – a shrine to what – to the Winter archivist? The Winters don't need any more shrines. They have a lifetime, three generations, of shrines, of institutes, of Versur, of the Hirschlich Centre, all of those things. We don't need any more shrines."

His pause was an invitation for Catherine to comment, but she slipped that chance and invited him instead to take a look round.

"Especially at the papers. I can't make head or tail of all these papers, but they seem somehow important."

"Yes, I should like very much to look through the papers of Ben. I hope that is acceptable. I believe I do need your permission as his executor, is that the right word. You have always been very honest about your role as the executor of his will. It was so typical of Ben. For him to ask you, really a stranger in so many ways. I do not mean to give offence. Let me say a recent acquaintance. Ben would prefer that. You cannot pry into his affairs. But I can. I do not want to and wish to avoid that. So for you to invite me to look at his papers, that is very important. I am not sure I express myself well."

She assured him he did. She did not disclose that prying was, now he used the term, exactly what she wanted him to do. She wanted to prise open the lid and discover the contents of this meticulously documented horde.

"It does not seem likely to me," Alain continued, "that Ben would have archived so much material – as you have described it to me. I still need to look directly at what is here. There are reasons. To do with the Winter Institute. When he left."

Catherine explained she needed to spend some minutes in the kitchen and asked him if he would excuse her and perhaps use the time to begin perusing the various papers. She topped up his glass, expensive St Emilion, and retreated to the kitchen.

By the time she had made the gravy, cooked the vegetables and served everything up, including a golden turkey crown ready to be carved, more than half an hour had passed. She had pulled out the small table at one side of the room and placed two fold away chairs from her Crouch End flat beside it. She had cleared the table earlier, except for the vase of flowers. This too now had to be moved to fit everything else on the crowded table top. She spooned cranberry jelly into another little bowl and found a teaspoon to serve it. The entire enterprise stretched the resources of the little kitchen to the extreme. Every pot, bowl, plate, glass and piece of cutlery was in use. She poured two glasses of a carefully chilled Meursault to accompany the meal. The table was worthy of a picture. She went to find Alain.

Alain was sat on Ben's bed. He had a small number of the files and a collection of the index cards beside him. He was intent. He looked up when she entered the room.

"Dinner? This is interesting. I did not know this existed. If you sell the flat, we must keep all these documents somehow." He followed her back into the living room.

"The table is exquisite, the aroma enticing. Dinner looks so delicious."

It was delicious. Alain was keen to talk. The papers had certainly acted as a stimulant to his usually calm persona.

He wanted to know what Catherine intended to do with Alain's things, with what he called the archive he had left.

She answered in her usual way.

"What do you think I should do with them?"

"As I said, they must be preserved. This is a unique record of the Winter Institute."

She wondered if she could just return them to the Institute. This drew almost a rebuke from Alain.

"No, that would be a mistake. I think it would be a betrayal to Ben. Ben left these papers for some reason. It would be a good reason. Let me take you to the times when I met Ben after he had left the Institute. Over five or six years ago. That is my guess. Perhaps it was an even longer time since he went from the Institute. We met in Lyon. Lyon was neutral for the Institute. The other places, of course, Versur itself but also Grenoble and Venice, they were all tainted. Is that the word I mean? They carried some sense of the Institute's influence. That sounds a little odd to you? Well, remember in Venice even, the Hirschlich Centre was a powerful part of the city. It boasted good visitor numbers and acted as a complement to the historic artistic attractions. The Winters always combined wealth with influence. That was their power – through their foundations and scholarships, the

Institute itself and the Centre – they had a network that reached deeply into European culture.

"Ben and I met in a favourite restaurant of his in the old town. It was winter – cold with sleety rain falling. I always find it difficult to imagine Lyon in the snow and cold when it is essentially still a Roman city. The restaurant was inexpensive. It reflected Ben's taste for something essential to the place but without affectation. He disliked the idea of Michelin stars that has now so overtaken the world.

"We ate *salade Lyonnaise* and *andouillette* and drank red house wine. It was rustic and rich. He was staying in his usual choice of hotel, two stars, shabby, central. It was about finishing up. I had been travelling to see him each day for a week after he had retired. We were exploring Lyon together. That day we had intended to visit Vienne. It was so rainy we decided against it and lunched in the old town. For Ben, I think this week in Lyon, it was a step to coming back here, to this flat. I hesitate to call it Ben's home. It is the place to which he returned.

"We were always more colleagues than friends, so it was unusual for us to socialise in this way. Yet, the place – Lyon itself and this particular restaurant – entirely spoke of Ben and who he was. Self-effacing, I believe that is the correct term. It entirely summed him up, but, of course, you knew him yourself, so you must have seen that."

Catherine nodded for it was true. Ben always preferred filter coffee or expresso to the fancier types, always preferred small, rather rundown cafes instead of the bland chains.

"We ate heartily, as I say. Ben asked after me. He warned me against ever living on the campus in Versur. I assured him that I would continue to live in Grenoble whatever I was offered by the Institute now he had retired. He nodded and said partly it was for my sake he wanted to meet. He called it a warning. 'Look at me as a warning,' he said, something like that.

"Because, and I knew this but no one had ever said it quite so distinctly, everyone at the Institute had an end date. Whatever you may believe in terms of loyalty to the Winters, there came a point when your services were no longer needed and instead you would be required to leave. We all knew this. Still, in that chilly day in Lyon and despite the good food and wine, it was, well, terrifying, to hear it spelt out so bluntly. Like hearing your fate being decided over which you have no control, no influence, because you have surrendered these things as part of your contract.

"I do not mean a contract of employment. Ben assured me that in his own case, and in every case he had experienced, the Institute went out of its way to be fair financially. There was, in fact, a beneficence in how the termination worked financially. A significant severance payment in addition to what was required legally and the real and enduring benefits of the generous pension made available from, in Ben's case, what now constituted early retirement.

"I am telling you this because Ben has left this flat to you for a reason. That is what I believe. He did not tell me this specifically. Now I have seen all these papers, well, it is what appears a reason. He went out of his way to seek your friendship?"

Catherine confirmed that was true. She thought it was so. After Alain had left, she went over this part again because it was important if Alain's insights were right. She thought it was true. Ben did seek her out. It was not just a chance acquaintance. He cultivated her. In some ways, he was always checking her out. She felt nothing sinister in understanding better that Ben's motives went deeper than wanting a companion for visits to museums and Italian conversation.

Catherine had asked Alain why he thought Ben hadn't told her about his other motives.

"Perhaps he hadn't known how to. He did not mean to die quite so abruptly, do you think? He was working on it. Maybe he wasn't quite ready to trust you so entirely, or maybe he hadn't found a way of telling you whatever it was he wanted you to do. Perhaps he did not know.

"In the Lyon restaurant I found him direct. Now, on reflection, the directness appears more a cover for being circumspect. The location, the neutral territory of Lyon, makes that clear. There was no danger of being overheard, spied on, bugged. Not that Versur is bugged. It is the sense of surveillance that permeates Versur; the sense that it is owned by the Institute and everything and everyone there is part of the Institute's programme. However progressive that programme may be, it still remains an issue of control. Ben was telling me to get ready to be gone myself. Not to become vulnerable to a sense of betrayal and loss. That is how he had found himself. That is what he said in Lyon."

Catherine thought about the Ben she had got to know. He was not a vulnerable man. He was self-effacing, just as Alain said, but also self-contained and sufficient to himself. Although by nature reticent, he had begun to speak a little about Claude, about losing Claude in the skiing accident. She hadn't pressed him on the matter. She felt he had mainly told her to provide a framework for his life story. He was an emotionally complete person. He did not require Catherine's active emotional engagement in his past losses and passions.

"What he told me, forcibly, was that I needed to make sure I had my own bolt hole. That is the term, because I did not immediately understand it and he had to explain – the place where the animal can run to when it is being hunted. That was another sinister idea. He only had his Bloomsbury bolt hole almost by chance. He told you about Claude?"

She nodded again. Yes, she knew the bare facts about Claude.

"Now we think nothing of two gay men in a relationship. Yet the Winter Institute was essentially conservative in outlook and solidly part of the establishment. When Ben and Claude first got together, any public acknowledgement of their relationship was impossible. Claude was the newly appointed director of the English Speaking Theatre. Naturally, being artistic, there was greater leeway in the attitude of the Institute. The Winters' paternalism went so far as to indulge as an acceptable folly Claude's sexuality. That indulgence was stretched a little when Claude struck up with the Winter archivist. It was acceptable so long as it was practised at some distance from the areas of influence. I don't think Herr Winter – the young Herr Winter – had even considered the possibility of Ben's sexuality. He was, after all, recruited as the archivist. What was acceptable in their social world proved less acceptable when it came to the staff, especially if it threatened the reputation and influence of the Institute. It amuses me to think of Ben and Claude as members of staff. I tell you truly we were all in livery. I think that is the correct expression.

"This is why Ben bought Bloomsbury – this flat. This was where he and Claude could live safely away from the intensity of Versur. They would come here between the productions at the English Speaking Theatre. Ben was circumspect about Bloomsbury. He would disappear. He took on projects with the archive which meant he preferred to work away from Versur. He needed access to libraries and records and London was often the place he needed to be, for the British Library and the Courtauld and the like. It worked perfectly and discreetly. What he indicated to me in Lyon was that I too needed a bolt hole. He told me he thought I knew this. I kept living in Grenoble. I had the excuse that it is after all my home. Ben didn't know if it was sufficient. It might not be a bolt hole. It was too close. After all, it was in the Winter's merchant house that the Institute had been started by Herr Winter senior. That is why I now have the apartment in Grenoble. A bolt hole, but a little too close for comfort. Nonetheless, I love Grenoble."

She asked him about Ben's recent visit to Grenoble, about why Alain had come back to London with him. Were there going to be any clues?

"Ben didn't look for clues. He was, like me, an archivist. He assembled documents. What he knew was that the documents did not add up. It bothered him. I had not realised for how long it had bothered him. He was, well, a little secretive."

She recognised the truth of this for sure. Yet she also saw it more as reticence. She observed Alain was agitated. He had moved on to the Meursault. He commented favourably on both wines.

"You say he spoke little of Claude. Yet Claude was the great emotional event of his life, the reason he bought this flat. The flat you now own. So that he and Claude could have a refuge from Versur, from the Institute. A place where they could love each other without the prying censoriousness of Versur and of the time.

"Ben would speak to me of the day Claude came to Versur, it must have been at the end of the eighties or the start of the nineties, before I worked there. I never knew Claude, but I heard about him from Ben. Ben told me, a rare thing for Ben, that Claude came in the summer. It was a wonderful summer. The French news was full of the much anticipated wonderful vintage. Everyone in Versur relaxed in the glorious sunshine and heat. He remembered the cafes spilling across the pavements with everyone drinking rosé. In the centre of the Versur campus there was a fountain. It is still there. It is an ugly, bronze thing, in the shape of flowers with animals cavorting around it. The children were running in and out of the fountain. They watched them as they drank their rosé, their mothers, seated at other tables, unconcerned that their little ones were sopping wet as they dried so quickly in the beautiful sunshine. This was the world Claude joined and he made it even more beautiful and glorious. Ben told me he could not hope to help me imagine what a beautiful and wonderful man Claude was and how his arrival was the moment of Versur's greatness.

"Herr Winter, of course, had secured Claude's services, stealing him from under the eyes of the theatre authorities in Paris. He was controversial. He challenged the daring and avant-garde. Now he was to be the Director of the Versur English Speaking Theatre. This was extraordinary. Why would a person of Claude's reputation and talent agree to take on a tiny theatre in a French backwater? Herr Winter was persuasive. He was also rich and generous. He had the great skill of combining a genuine appreciation with the support of apparently limitless wealth. Claude would not be directing an obscure theatre in a French backwater; he would become part of the great Winter Institute. His productions would be premiered here, but then after Grenoble and Venice become touring phenomena across the world. The greatest actors would seek to work with him.

"Claude moved to Versur. Just like the rest of us, he became part of the Institute's family. He enjoyed all the privileges we had become used to – the rent free apartments, the freedom over our time and activities, the cultural life of the Institute in Versur and beyond. He became a symbol of that culture. His daring productions, the great actors he was able to attract as well as designers, composers. Legendary was Herr Winter's intention and for a time it was legendary; had the potential to be so. That is why even I, now all this time later feel sad the English Speaking Theatre closed its doors. It was like a little death of Versur, a life limiting stroke."

Catherine tried to think of Versur and Claude, to imagine through Alain's eyes, that scene, what, 25 more than 25 years ago. It sounded possible. Ben was not a romantic, but she had found him to be more than sympathetic, to have a deep seated sense of the emotional. Ben had been real to her like one of her pots, one of her best pots.

Alain was agitated. The story had excited him. The past came back vividly. He was unable to remain seated. He went over to the desk and began again to finger the index cards still on the desktop after he had taken them out of the drawers. The evening had passed quickly. The excitement of seeing Ben's archive, the food, the exhilaration of revisiting the past.

"May I just again look through some of Ben's records? I shall need to go soon. Tomorrow I return to Grenoble. I hope that you will visit me there. We can go to Versur, although it is now a different Versur however much Herr Winter may wish to maintain the legend of the Winter Institute."

She nodded. She was mesmerised by all of this. The clues to what mystery or crime, she did not know. First, why was she the sudden inheritor of Ben's life? Secondly, what was she supposed to do with all of these records? The legacy was not simply property that needed to be disposed of and the proceeds distributed. It was an archive. She thought of it as an alternative archive. The Winter's archivist's personal archive, a counter archive. She had no idea of how to access the archive. Could she seriously imagine herself reading these documents, somehow assembling from them the story Ben could not himself piece together?

Alain returned from the bedroom. He held a pamphlet. It was faded but otherwise in perfect condition. It looked unread. He held it up.

"Look, this is great. I had hoped to find this in any case amongst his things. This is the introduction Ben wrote to Versur. He wrote it soon after he was appointed. He often spoke about it and for a time it was the essential guide to Versur. It was freely distributed so that any visitor had one. That is why it is a relatively brief pamphlet."

Catherine asked him if he would like to have it.

"No, I have one of my own, but I think if you read this, that would get you started. It would be a good starting point."

She looked at him blankly and he correctly interpreted her expression and laughed.

"A starting point for your work – the job Ben has given you. You are to be the author of the history Ben could never write. You are the objective observer who will tell the story Ben has left you in all of these carefully catalogued records. You will become the historian that we the archivists work for. Congratulations!"

Alain left soon afterwards. It was later than Catherine realised. Too late for her to feel comfortable returning home on the 91 bus. She would have to stay the night here. An unplanned first night in Ben's flat. She and Alain had agreed to keep in touch by Skype. She had told him she needed time to think and to reflect on what he had said. The evening was, she thought, a success. Now she felt tired. Alain's enthusiasm, his descriptions of golden Versur, of golden Claude, left her with a sense of greater loss in Ben's death. The night would be edgy. It was a night for reflection, for thought about what she did next. Alain had been pleased with the pot she had made for him which she gave him having emptied it of the few remaining uneaten Brussel sprouts and quickly rinsed it clean. She wrapped it in some brown paper and he took it like that.

Next day, she took the guide with her back to her home in Crouch End. She needed to get back to her own life. She even thought of finding Kate the student to talk to her about the success, she thought of it as a success, of her dinner with Alain.

Welcome to wonderful Versur! We have written this brochure to introduce you to our beautiful town and as a guide to some of its main attractions. As a visitor we want you to have the opportunity to enjoy all of our attractions and understand a little about how and why Versur is such a treasured town.

When we speak of Versur we must naturally also speak of the Winter Institute. The Institute and the town are as one, linked by a history of shared resources and aspirations. Originally based in the trading house of Herr Winter senior in Grenoble, the Institute moved its main base to Versur in 1948. Herr Winter senior at the age of 41 and in response to the terrible events of the war gave up his mercantile career to hand himself over entirely to the affairs of the Institute. The Institute as you must already know exists to promote peaceful relations in Europe and beyond through culture and the arts. It retained its office in Grenoble, now used for teaching and as a residence for the Winter family, and since 1955 has exhibited Herr Winter's outstanding collection of early twentieth-century art at the Hirschlich Centre in Venice.

The Winter Institute has invested heavily in the town of Versur as an example of how cooperation and culture can create a unique ambience for peaceful coexistence and community. This has most famously extended to the legendary English Speaking Theatre. It also supports the local schools, the Winter Institute Art College but also the sports facilities and local football team. A healthy approach to physical exercise alongside our unique cultural centres creates what Herr Winter junior has called, the Versur effect.

When you first arrived in Versur you would not have been struck by anything out of the ordinary. Versur is a typical, quaint town or village in the Rhône-Alpes. It has a weekly market in the narrow main street where there are two cafes and, at the furthest end, a hotel in the former small chateau. The hotel has an excellent restaurant which modestly boasts one Michelin star. The houses are mainly of the Alpine chalet style common in these parts. Most were built in the first part of the century and several date back in to the nineteenth and even eighteenth centuries. The town soon peters out into countryside. It is constrained from growing by the steep hills within which the valley it inhabits lies. When I asked Herr Winter senior why he had singled out Versur for the great privilege of being the new home for the Winter Institute, he told me this was where the Winter family had its summer home. In fact, the summer home was on the same spot as where we find the contemporary buildings of the Institute. These are modern. It is true that when they were erected in the late forties, there was controversy surrounding the uncompromising modernity of the architecture. Now this seems strange, as the buildings – characterised by a style recognisable to students of Le Corbusier – seem part and parcel of the quaintness and attractions of Versur. Indeed, they appear to me to emerge from the countryside in a most attractively deceptive manner. A gaunt reminder of civilisation against the grandeur of the elements.

I cannot now restrain myself from jumping in and telling you about the English Speaking Theatre. As a relative newcomer to the Winter Institute, like you, I suspect this famous institution is one of the main attractions of Versur. So I was surprised to learn that it had happened almost as an accident. Throughout Herr Winter senior's childhood – itself punctuated by the horror of the Great War – his family had supported an annual four week run of a play in English at the theatre in Grenoble. It was this family tradition that Herr Winter wanted to build on – but how to do this?

In drawing up the architectural plans for the Institute, the decision was made to create a lecture space. That was the point at which Herr Winter realised that a theatre – a permanent theatre – as part of the Institute made the most sense and it would be English speaking as part of that childhood family tradition and in respect for the great drama of the English speaking world.

Catherine stopped reading. She looked at the title page to see when the *Guide to Versur (English version)* had been published. The date given was 1981. A year after Ben said he had started working there at the age of 24.

They had been having coffee in the restaurant in the new wing of the National Gallery. Stuck inside the café, as the tables with views of Trafalgar Square were restricted to diners only, she had listened to Ben speaking about his job as Winter Archivist. She was surprised now to be able to recall quite so much of what he had said. It seemed then to be of no particular interest, except it told her about him.

Ben spoke with an unusual degree of excitement. Catherine watched and listened as he told her of his excitement to be appointed as archivist to the Winter Institute. She lied when he asked her how much she knew of its work. She had never heard of it. Her fascination was to be slowly uncovering in this new acquaintance a better understanding of who he really was. Her mind, partly translating some of the pots from the Dutch paintings they had been studying to her own studio, heard him talking with this enthusiasm for an Institute.

He was so young and it was such a wonderful opportunity. He loved the idea of living abroad, especially in Versur itself. She also lied when he asked her if she had visited the Hirschlich Centre in Venice. She had not wanted to visit, she recalled, as she had so little time and Venice seemed an odd place to seek out modern art.

Ben's memories of the early years of his time there were joyous. His face had become so animated as they drank their filter coffees. Ben's dislike of any other sort of coffee, to Catherine's annoyance, remembered also by Alain.

They ordered another coffee and Catherine paid. Ben was concerned he was boring her talking so much about himself. He wasn't and she told him. He looked grateful and sensed permission to continue. He wanted to speak more about the earlier years. Later, he said, it had gone wrong. He wasn't specific. Everything comes to an end and not always well. That had been Catherine's experience. Sitting across from him, she felt he was something special although for her the time for anything other than acquaintance was decisively over. She did not have the time, the energy, the inclination. It allowed her to understand that she had never really had the inclination to be in love, to have a relationship. Just, younger, she supposed she was meant to; the way you are meant to have children.

Ben had stopped talking and Catherine realised it was because she had gone off on these thoughts of her own. Tentatively, she spoke out loud to Ben about her lack of inclination for love. That was when he had spoken of Claude, his great friend, lover and partner and the reason for buying the flat in Bloomsbury. He spoke in such a way that Catherine understood he did not wish to dwell on this topic. It was out of a sympathy with her own feelings, or lack of them. Perhaps to say, it is possible, upon an occasion, to be wrong about inclinations. It would be possible to fall in love. He had said that.

They finished their second cup of coffee and it was the right moment, on that note, for them to leave. They walked together down the grand staircase and left through the revolving door. It was a dry day. She was making for the bus stop. The 91 bus as ever she recalled amused. Then he realised he had forgotten his umbrella in the restaurant. She offered to go back with him to find it but he said no, he didn't want to delay her, so she had carried on to the bus stop. She didn't know if he had found the umbrella.

She thought now, reading the Guide he had written, she would need to recall all those meetings. There probably weren't that many. The outing to Walworth. The various coffees. The conversations in which she had learned a little of Ben. Yet the puzzle of why he had left all his worldly belongings to her remained. If it was a puzzle. The sense of loss grew, she discovered, the more she remembered of what he had said, the more she went to his flat.

She was going there a lot more. She spent one or two nights there each week now. The rhythm of her days was altered. At first she saw it as a disruption, like an illness or the visit of a friend, that would come to an end and routine would return. It was not like that, or if it was an illness it was one that developed. Illness was the wrong thing. It appeared now to her more like a pot. It was a pot she could imagine, that she could build layer upon layer – an enormous, uncontrollable pot.

Her own potting had halted. This upset her less than she thought. Before when these interruptions came they caused her severe upset. She sought help from other potters, from counsellors. She feared a block that cut her off creatively, her natural element taken away from her. Now, especially when she was sitting at the desk in Ben's flat reading through various documents, she felt an intense sense of being. It superseded her need to pot.

At the community college she collected a couple of the slab pots that were now fired and finished. She was seeking Kate. She had decided to act on her desire to discuss what was going on and why not Kate. She found she was really quite fond of Kate as far as people, acquaintances go. Just like she had with Ben.

Kate was found as usual working on her pots in the studio. She asked to look at the work Catherine had bubble wrapped and put in her hessian bag. She unwrapped it and left it for Kate to consider. She knew Kate worked almost entirely in slab and she knew her own pots were not what she had wanted to achieve.

Kate looked at them inquisitively. They surprised Kate. Surprised because she told her Catherine was for her, Kate, an inspiration and a wonderful teacher. She didn't comment on the two pots Catherine had unwrapped. Instead she began to speak about her own pots; about how slab was to do with counter levering mass. It was creating the sense of body and weight – not denying the quality of heaviness – with deftness. Slab turned artifice on its head because it relied on honesty.

They talked about what Catherine should work on next. Catherine asked Kate what she thought she should do. Kate was reticent. It was, she supposed, about change. Catherine agreed. The change had happened to her – Ben and all that – and at the same time as her long running creative streak had finally petered out. Like a student again, she needed to find a beginning. She was not moving on but starting out on something. Kate asked Catherine what she thought of the slab pots they were still both looking at. Catherine laughed and wrapped them up. She had decided and was grateful to Kate for being round about, a friend.

She left the pots still wrapped and in the bag at her Crouch End flat before putting some more of her clothes into a rucksack and heading off for Ben's flat. It was already the afternoon and she knew she would be staying overnight again there. On arrival she switched on the computer and looked at her emails. One from Ben's solicitor immediately caught her attention. It was the final statement of the estate, his bill and an attachment with the land registry entry for the flat in her name. That was how it happened. Catherine had expected there to be meetings, discussions, telephone conversations but there had been nothing after the first meeting, just papers sent through that needed to be signed. Fortunately, Ben's savings had covered the inheritance tax bill leaving her now the owner in her own name of his flat. There wasn't much other money left over. She was grateful for this. The flat was too much. Having Ben's cash would have felt immoral, wrong, soiled.

She made a coffee and felt at home. She had begun systematically to look through the throngs of records. Her approach, after reading The Guide, was to sample a particular document, folder, notebook or file from each section of Ben's archive. She quickly discovered that for each item there was a corresponding index card and the index cards were also grouped by categories such as Hirschlich Centre, Art Works,

Winter Senior, Winter Junior. The increased familiarity with this contained work comforted her even as the sense of loss increased. She knew, of course, that she would never see Ben again just as she would never see her mother or father again. This had never before phased her. People close to her faded but were remembered. Others were forgotten completely. The difference with Ben was that she urgently needed to meet up with him. She had quite a few questions where he would be invaluable in filling gaps in her knowledge. So it really was more than inconvenient that he hadn't been around a bit longer to solve parts of the mystery.

Executing the will was chillingly straightforward. No more difficult than packing up Ben's clothes and having them collected by the British Heart Foundation. Not so Ben's emails and internet accounts. She had first attempted to have these transferred so that she could use his router and WIFI. Hopeless. She had to open a new account, the one she was now using to read her own emails. His emails had died with him. Alain said he used the email very little and almost entirely for practical arrangements. From the contents of his flat it was clear it relied on the physical record. Yet somewhere his email account carried on. How many emails each day are received by the dead. The offers of reduced price shoes or train tickets or meals continuing unabated.

She sat with her coffee on the sofa reading the latest sample from the record. It was entitled, File Note after Meeting with Herr Winter re Draft of Versur Guide. It was dated 1981. A year after Ben had taken the job at the Winter Institute, when he was 24.

Herr Winter communicated to me that the paragraphs about the social purpose of the Winter Institute's presence in Versur were not quite right. He kindly praised the quality of the prose and my ability quickly to understand the Institute. However, I had misunderstood. Versur was not in any way a 'social experiment', the term I had used in the draft of the Versur Guide. 'Experiment', he commented, suggested something being tried out to see whether or not it worked. That was not how the Institute's support of Versur had come about. It was instead a vision of how a community could be; of the desire of the Winter family to use its wealth to benefit Versur in a quite specific way. Versur is an alternative approach. It cannot be validated through an experiment any more than an individual life is an experiment that can be repeated. This is it; this is the Versur the Winters wish to create.

As with many of the records, a post-it note had been attached with a handwritten note. This one was dated 2013, two years after Ben retired from the Winter Institute.

It is interesting to me that my naivety in recording uncritically Herr Winter (this was Herr Winter junior, I believe) hid from me any suspicion that this was typical of the way in which Versur became part of the Winter psyche. That projection, paid for it is true with their money, now seems to me increasingly sinister although I do not exactly know why I choose the word sinister to describe it. There was nothing fundamentally wrong with the Institute or Versur, and yet now all these years later it strikes me as sinister. I was caught up entirely in that world, believing in the goodness of the Winters and wholeheartedly embracing their vision and ideals.

The Skype call with Alain was scheduled for the same evening. When they connected, Catherine could see Alain with a glass of wine relaxing in his Grenoble flat. It was still winter although Christmas had come and gone as Catherine part moved into Ben's flat. Alain wore a patterned jumper in a thick wool yarn. It made him look kind and generous. He had just filled his glass before the call, he said.

Catherine asked him if he had read his emails and, of course, he had not. She had sent him a copy of the record she had been reading that afternoon and the attached post-it note.

When, after fumbling with the computer in front of him, Alain had had the chance to read the papers she had sent. He looked up, surprised.

"I should not be surprised," he started, "this is the same way he spoke when we met after he left the Institute. It is the same he was saying when he visited me here just at the end of last year before he died so suddenly. It is more interesting, I think, because he uses the documents he has kept from the past."

Catherine explained there were many similar documents, although she had read only samples from different parts of the archive. She knew what he would say. That she was the historian who would unlock the work of the archivist. She asked him bluntly how and he shrugged and said to her to keep in touch because she would figure that out. They signed off warmly.

Slab pottery, all pottery went on hold. Catherine gave herself a year. She would write the history of the Winter

Archivist. She would become the Winter Archivist, not Ben. She would create her potted version of who he had been and what he had discovered. Now, she thought. I'll start writing tonight. It will be Ben's autobiography. She would become his ghost writer, the ghost of the Winter Archivist writing his own autobiography. I, Ben, the Winter Archivist arrived in Versur newly appointed, naïve, excited, ready for my career and my life, ready for anything.

Part Two

Leipzig 1985

I remember the place. It was before the fall of the wall was even imaginable. Or at least only imaginable in the heads of crackpots. The building was, like the city itself, concrete, grey. I felt suspicion. People did not look at me. I was avoided. I looked different. My clothes, my worn but expensive winter coat, my shoes – highly polished expensive. All of these indicated I was not of the place. Not a visitor but an interloper who could never belong. I had expected the suspicion of the authorities, and I was not wrong there. I had not expected the suspicion of everyone I met. The waiters obliged to serve me in chilly, large dining rooms that resembled public execution chambers. A crystal chandelier providing a sense of luxury only emphasising its want. Suspicion was in the street. I felt observed and later found out that throughout my trip I was observed. I had no choice but to come here. When I spoke to Herr Winter about it, the younger Herr Winter who was my boss but also so much more, he called it field work. For ease, let me say when I refer to Herr Winter in these notes, I always mean the younger Herr Winter. If I shall need to speak about Herr Winter senior, I shall always refer to him as the Herr Winter senior. Yes, that is very appropriate.

It felt like field work. I felt like a spy. I felt like a spy because everyone in Leipzig, in the whole of the East, assumed I was a spy. There was no other meaningful reason for a westerner to make this trip. Only spying made sense to a community corroded and glued together by suspicion.

That was the first night. I had booked four. My visa allowed me to travel by train from West Germany only to Leipzig and to stay four nights. I had requested longer. That had been refused. The embassy in Zurich, where I had waited many hours on subsequent days, helped me little. I was made to understand that this was a great privilege, four days. My nationality didn't help. An Englishman living in France on some hare brained sounding excursion to identify a German from before the war now dead.

Herr Hirschlich, I had explained, was an art dealer who had disappeared during the war. He was Jewish, so it was easy to jump to the conclusion he had lost his life as part of the Holocaust. Yet, I explained further, I had failed to turn up any trace of him in the extensive records kept by his supposed torturers and murderers. This was unusual. I explained, I laughed a little to make myself human, that I too was a record keeper, and archivist, in fact the archivist for the Winter Institute of which I am sure they would have heard.

The official, the man, poorly dressed, overweight, apparently uninterested in himself and certainly not me, yawned his disapproval at my verbosity. Specifically, he asked, why did I need to visit Leipzig. The question meant why did this spy need to go to Leipzig. He took my answer in good part. He asked me to return the next day. His secretary, who sat taking notes throughout our meeting, accompanied me into the neighbouring office. A time was booked. There was no small talk.

So the visa was granted. Later in the trip I would discover from my overseer that the reason was to find an answer to why this spy needed to visit Leipzig. That was all. He believed me right away when I told him I was looking for records of the birth of Herr Hirschlich. That was later in the trip. For now I was still gaining access to the records.

The building in Leipzig sat slanting to the road. I doubted it was completely new. Some kind of entrance annex had been constructed which provided this strange diagonal of grey concrete, bunker like, into which doors had been punched as if hit by tank rounds. The city, I observed, had been both cleared of war debris and up to a point rebuilt. Still the war lingered here. It was an atmospheric affect, a failure to forget, or to allow memory to fade. Instead here it lingered as a borrowed thought of what might have happened – and now happily, has.

The new entrance, lent on to the old brick built building, provided the unheated waiting room where a few of us sat in our coats – mine noticeably better and warmer than the others there. A man sat behind the low reception desk where we gave our names on arrival in the morning. When it was my turn to be seen, a woman came to fetch me and accompanied me to the particular office to see the official designated to deal with this case. I followed her the first day into the older building. The corridors were featureless, simply providing access on right and left to small box like offices. The wooden doors to each office had a small glass panel allowing you to see inside as you walked down the corridor. As I walked the length of the first corridor, a single stride behind the female assistant, I peered in. Each office was the same. A single window, a desk with a chair in front of it. A light on the desk. Most of the offices were unoccupied. Occasionally, I could see someone sat behind one of the desks, head bent over, writing. Once, someone was sitting on the chair in front of the desk with their back to me – man or woman, I could not tell, in conversation with a man behind the desk. Mainly, however, the rooms were empty. As we reached the end of this corridor I realised the absence. There were no computers. Just a desk, a light, two chairs one behind, one in front of the desk.

We turned right at the end of the corridor and a small hallway opened before us. Here there were two lifts. They most resembled the sort of lifts you find in hotels for ferrying goods to the kitchen. Each had an accordion style metal panel door. She pressed the call button. She had not spoken beyond a single command in German. We waited and the lift arrived slowly and noisily. It took us to the next floor, so I wondered why we did not use the stairs. The office, similar to all of those on the ground floor, was close to the lift, but in a corridor at a 35 degree angle to the one below. The geography of the building had been confused by the strange entrance area. I now understood, the lift was in the original entrance area and three corridors led off this like spokes in a wheel. We had entered the building from the back.

This was the first day. I must make the most of each day, I remember thinking as I sat down. "Herr Wilkins, willkommen," the official behind the desk had said. Wilkins pronounced Vilkins.

I had said thank you and ventured a "Herr?" but no name was forthcoming. The woman accompanying me seated herself behind me on the only other available chair by the door. I had not seen the third chair peering in from the corridor to each office as it was hidden behind the door itself. I knew that every office would be furnished in exactly the same way.

The unnamed official was gracious by the standards of the place and we spoke in English. I complimented him on his English and excellent accent. He smiled and this was a welcome change from the normal although he was quick to return to his official look combining a frown with a sense of impatience reserved for a wayward child.

Our interview lasted for over an hour. I do still think that he wanted to practise his English and therefore kept me longer than otherwise. The woman remained silent except for an occasional cough. My request was unusual. In preparation for my visit, a preliminary search had been made of the records. No records for a Matthau Hirschlich had been found, or even for a family of that name in the Leipzig area. Of course, understandably, many records had been lost and destroyed in the course of the war. Nonetheless, many remained. It was strange that, if this man had been a reasonably successful business man in the twenties and thirties, there was no trace.

I explained that Herr Hirschlich, from what we understood at the Winter Institute, had moved his business to Berlin in the early thirties. He had been associated with the artists exhibited at the Nazis Degenerate Art Exhibition. He would have been targeted, we believed, by the Nazis early on both as an art dealer and as a Jew.

The man shrugged. Maybe he was tired with the West's obsession with the Holocaust. In the East they could see life over the border daily on TV. Why be so concerned about the past when life in the present was so good. I asked if I could examine the records myself. I gave my credentials as a professional archivist. These appeared to impress him. He suggested I return the following day. By then the decision would have been made about what and how I might be allowed to see. I asked him when I should return and who I should ask for. He smiled. The same time. I would be expected. I did not need the official's name.

The woman stood behind me. The first interview was over. I abandoned any further attempts at conversation and followed the woman as we retraced our steps to the entrance hall where she left me. I bade her farewell in English and she nodded, from which I understood her to understand our previous conversation. It crossed my mind whether the assistant, as I had assumed her to be, was in fact more of an overseer. Everyone listened in to everyone else. Everyone was a potential informer. No one was above suspicion. No one could be trusted.

I stepped out of the building and buttoned my coat as the cold abruptly greeted me. I should have worn a hat. Outside, the fresh air reminded me of the ubiquitous tobacco fumes inside the building. Everyone smoked. The receptionist, the woman assistant or overseer, the man who had interviewed me. Stale smoke was the flavour of the interiors of Leipzig. It felt like a veil of smog across the poorly furnished and inadequately heated government buildings. Pleasant as it was to breath fresh air, it was too cold to linger for very long out of doors. I now had the rest of the day and the evening to fill. I returned to my hotel. At the reception I asked for a city map. The woman on the desk asked me to wait. She picked up the phone and rang someone. I sat on the false leather sofa that was the only piece of seating available despite the quite large lobby of the hotel's modern building. Here at least I could relax and review the morning's meeting. I had no idea whether I was making any progress, or whether I was truly on a wild goose chase in my search for information about Matthau Hirschlich. I would have liked a coffee, but the cafeteria area where the breakfast had been served – a slice of bread and some tinned mini hot dog sausages with grey coloured mustard – was closed. I wasn't sure what I intended to do for lunch and dinner.

I waited patiently. I was resting really. The hour with the East German official, overseen by the woman assistant had tired me more than I had expected. After a certain time, I am not sure how long as I partly rested as well as considered my options for the next three days, another man, quite a young man, arrived. His English was also excellent. He had come in response to the call from the woman at the hotel desk. He explained, her English was limited – as was my German I apologised. He understood that I wanted a city map. He wondered if he might in fact be able to help. Could he perhaps give me a tour of the city? He was not from Leipzig himself. He lived in Berlin, but he was happy to be of service and show me the several wonderful things here. Also, he would be happy to take me to an excellent restaurant for some lunch.

I asked him bluntly if he was my minder. Then, at the expression of slight anguish on his face, regretted the rudeness of my question. I immediately apologised. This cheered him up and elicited the reply that here things happened in a certain way to which I would need to become accustomed. I reached out my hand to shake his and he was prompt to respond. After the handshake, I was equally quick to accept his kind offer of a city tour and lunch.

In fact, we lunched first. The morning had passed already and I was quite ready for something to eat. The restaurant served traditional Saxon food. There was a table cloth. I declined the offer of wine. As well as mashed potato, the dish consisted of a slice of some sort of luncheon meat, smothered in a fairly thin gravy with a fried egg on top. There didn't appear to be a menu, just the dish of the day which we both ate. My new companion ate carefully, slowly, savouring the meal. I found the gravy greasy and the meat slithery on the tongue with little flavour other than salt. We had coffee and I thanked the man for helping me during my stay. He smiled. I offered to pay, but he would not allow me to, saying I was a guest and he wanted me to see the city at its best.

We saw the Bach church, the St Nicholas Church and the old town hall. He left me for a time in the museum, with its uneven collection of paintings and historical artefacts. Then we finished by visiting a park and gardens. It was colder now the sun was setting. The man looked cold. I remember the trip very well. I have revisited Leipzig again of course since reunification. I have imagined that air of suspicion, of half of the people checking what the other half were doing, but no one knowing which half was which. The stale smoke in every room and building and the food which was hard to digest and didn't fill you up. I remember it fondly like a school trip you took because it was the school trip and no other reason.

It was just after five when we returned to the hotel. We had been on foot since lunch and in the cold weather I was now really quite tired. I was ready to retire to my room. I imagined I would get something to eat in the hotel cafeteria, although it remained stubbornly closed as we stood in the hotel lobby. I was keen to thank my guide – name unknown.

He was looking around for something. He asked me to wait there. He went behind the reception desk to use the phone. As he replaced the receiver, he held his hand up. Across the lobby another man who had just entered from the street raised his hand in turn.

"Herr Wilkins," he said by way of introduction, "this is Willi. Willi will look after you this evening. My time with you is over and I hope you have enjoyed the lunch and the beautiful city."

We shook hands for the second time.

"Thank you. I will help Herr Wilkins from here." Willi said Wilkins in the English pronunciation. My tour guide left us. I realised that unlike the escapades at the records office, the tour guide had not himself had a minder. Nor would it appear had Willi.

I have this picture still of first meeting Willi in the hotel lobby, his hand raised in greeting and salute to the tour guide. Willi who was yet to find out the extent to which his world would change. He knew more than most, or was prepared to examine the possibility in 1985 of the world of East Germany as he knew it, as he had grown up with it, changing. He was dismissive of the tour guide when we spoke later that evening. The tour guide was from Berlin, so he thought he was top of the class, and probably was, but in Leipzig, which was Willi's home, there was more afoot. Willi was very open. I wondered why he felt the confidence not to succumb to the need to observe and be observed, to suspect and be suspected. Leipzig, he explained, was at the edge of what the authorities were willing to tolerate in terms of challenges to the system. The reason he could entertain the possibility of political change, which even he could not afford to acknowledge outside an unvoiced, unstructured feeling was that he saw first-hand how uncertain the authorities were how to respond to the challenges they were experiencing in Leipzig. All of this could not be spoken about. It could not be written down. There were no documents. Willi couldn't even think about it, just feel. Thoughts can be policed, because thoughts are the triggers for suspicion. Only feelings, unexplained and inarticulate, enabled Willi to see into a very different future.

I trusted Willi because he told me straight after the tour guide left that I could not trust him. He knew I knew this, but when he looked after western guests, he was always surprised how slow they were to learn that this was a practical skill. For him, for the tour guide, for everyone I met in East Germany, not trusting people was the skill they all learned from birth. It was the foundation of the Party's power and surpassed any individual's power. It was overwhelming.

So I trusted him. I told him of my faux pas, asking the tour guide if he was my minder, and Willi roared with laughter – he actually roared, like a wild animal. That is Willi. So large, so confident, so definite. He dismissed the man again. He's from Berlin, and laughed loudly again. The only person I had met in the East to laugh out loud. That was how confident Willi felt.

He took me to dinner. He asked me if I liked sauerkraut. I nodded appreciatively. He told me I needed to get better at lying if I was intending to stay here much longer. No one outside Germany likes sauerkraut. Sauerkraut is like communism. Only people in communist countries like it. He laughed. That is mainly what I remember about that evening. Willi laughing. We drank a lot of Georgian champagne. I ate the sauerkraut. I assured Willi it was delicious. He told me I was beginning to sound like a communist. The soup like stew of meat, I admitted, was less delicious. No, I would never make it as a communist. I kept on wanting to get to the truth instead of the right answer.

When I remember Willi now, I see him across the table in the candlelight of what was I suspect the best restaurant in Leipzig. They knew him there. The second bottle of champagne was opened by one of the waiters and Willi looked so young. He could only have been thirty, if that. He spoke without caution, or so it seemed to me. Naturally, I adored him. I don't know what he felt. I think he did not know what he felt. Like suspicion, he had learned to feel without knowing. That would be a good question for him, feelings, how they operated.

He could not restrain himself from speaking about the East, about his love for communism, his irritation that Germany was always about the Holocaust – in the West, he meant. When he said Germany, he was always speaking about West Germany. The East for him then was communism. Communism, he meant this, was about the future. Germany always looked back, always handicapped by the war, by the Holocaust, by Nazism. It was 1985 and he wanted the future, the next century.

He was so open. Of course he worked for the State. Everyone worked for the State. His laughter enhanced by the champagne. His joke. Everyone worked for the State and all foreigners were spies. Did I really not understand this. The only reason a westerner would come to the East was to spy. He told me I would return to the West and tell lies about the terrible food, the constant minding by state officials, the bad clothes, the weather. The weather was not the fault of communism. Everything else, well, that was the plot by the West to undo communism.

He was drunk. We were both drunk. He escorted me back to the hotel. He asked if he could buy my coat. He would buy it with champagne, Georgian champagne, courtesy of the Communist Party. I offered to give it to him. No, he could not accept. They would see he had a coat from the West. He would be a class traitor. Hilarity illuminated his continuing conversation. Back at the hotel, he ordered coffee. At the desk the overnight clerk was full of sleep. He looked furtive as he took the order from Willi. Willi insisted the cafeteria be reopened; the cafeteria that had remained stubbornly closed since the breakfast. Willi acted like a drunk moneyed patron of a London nightclub. I said, I didn't need coffee, but it wasn't about coffee, it was about making the clerk do something. Willi could get things done. The padlocked chain was taken off the double doors leading into the large and featureless room. The lights were switched on. Some instant coffee, Kaffee-Mix, was produced. Then Willi stopped. He apologised to the clerk. The clerk just looked more scared by the apology than by Willi's drunken orders and demands.

"Don't drink the coffee."

Willi sounded sober now, emphatic. I was drunk, too drunk to understand. The clerk looked agitated and indicated to us to hurry up. He wanted to turn off the lights in the cafeteria and relock the doors. We were standing by the urn used to boil water. Willi still held the sachet of Kaffee-Mix. He held it like a connoisseur.

"It will poison you!"

Then the laugh, the loud laugh, and even the clerk smiled.

"He is not allowed to say that." Willi pointed at the clerk, who did not understand English. "I won't tell him in German. If I said our glorious instant coffee mix would poison us in German, I would be a state criminal. Then again we are all probably state criminals. We just haven't yet found out the crime we have committed. We have the rest of our lives to find that out. I can help with that."

The clerk was smiling. Smiling, I think, because Willi was laughing and he wanted to respond correctly. Willi put down the sachet.

"Let us postpone the poison until breakfast."

The clerk seeing Willi had apparently abandoned the coffee plan attempted to usher us back to the lobby out of the cafeteria. I knew this would be a mistake. Willi held up his hand. He held up his hand as he had held up his hand greeting the overseer from Berlin when we had first been introduced.

"*Wein,*" he commanded.

The clerk retreated to the door, his ushering attempt in abeyance. Willi followed him and I followed Willi. He turned to me in the doorway.

"No more wine," he said, "it is late and tomorrow, tomorrow we must both be archivists for the day."

We shook hands and Willi strode out of the hotel. At the revolving door he looked round. He laughed.

The clerk had retreated back behind the desk. He handed me my key. I never needed to give my name. I was a marked man. We said good night in German and I suppose the clerk must have shut up the cafeteria after I had gone. In the morning, it was open, breakfast was being served and after sleeping better than I imagined possible, I was looking forward to finding out what I could about Matthau Hirschlich.

In the cafeteria, Willi was sitting with a cup of coffee. He stood when I entered and welcomed me to the table.

"Our spy from the West," he greeted me.

I smiled but was uncertain at his manner.

"Now we are friends. In our cups. I am going to flee the East and join you in England. We are going to make a huge success of the future. First, let us research your Herr Hirschlich. Herr Hirschlich aus Leipzig, nein?"

We walked the short distance to the records office where I had met the official yesterday. We entered by the same public entrance. The same receptionist sat at the desk, but Willi took me straight past him and together without anyone else we went into the back to front building and this time took the worn out lift to the basement. Here were the records; literal, physical, records. A man was working at a desk in the centre of the room surrounded by the shelves of records. The shelves operated on some sort of system that allowed them to be stacked alongside each other. You could only access one row of records at a time, and to do so, each of the shelves had to be physically pulled across to allow you to enter. The man looked up and Willi introduced me to him. As always, no name was given. The only person whose name I knew was Willi.

The man indicated to me that I should sit beside him. Willi remained standing vaguely looking at the shelves of records and pushing one of the set of shelves to open up a new row. The man looked at him, irritated, but said nothing. In front of the man was a ledger of some sort which he opened at a page marked with a slip of paper. He invited me to look at what was written on the ledger page.

Now, of course, I would simply be able to photograph the page with a phone. Then there was no such technology. I had brought my simple camera with its 35mm roll of film. On the tour, my wish to use the camera had provoked concern from my guide. He permitted me to take pictures of the churches and of the town hall, but nothing else. He refused to have his own photo taken when I asked him to pose in front of St Thomas church. Instead, scanning the page the man indicated, I took out my notebook to copy into it what I could see there.

The ledger was some sort of city record of transactions, and the entry was for a licence to make changes to a building. The reason it was of interest is that the application had been made by one Herr Hirschlich. It gave his address. I carefully transcribed the details into my notebook. I also looked at the beginning of the ledger. It appeared to be one of a series in the city archives. I asked the man if I could see where it belonged in the archive. He looked at Willi who was still idling by the shelves. Willi came over. I could see a sense of boredom on his part. For once he was not smiling. Willi nodded when the man repeated my request to him in German.

The man led me further into the record store and manipulated the shelves with the sliding mechanism opening another row of records. We walked along this and came to the obvious gap left by the ledger which remained on the table behind us. I made to pull out the book preceding that volume and the man nodded his assent. It was too heavy to look at easily in the narrow space between the shelves so we took it back to the table. I inspected it. There was a numbering system that clearly indicated the book with the Hirschlich reference was the next in this series of records. The records all appeared to be related to building work, changes in structures and layouts. The entries were chronological. I asked Willi where the various streets were. Most he did not know. Small streets, he imagined. The street with the Hirschlich reference still existed. He had already checked. Many streets had been damaged or reordered after the war, so it was never easy to find these old addresses. It was not encouraged.

As far as my request to be left to go through the records myself, this was denied. There was no possibility that someone like me would be let loose in the Leipzig city records. The authorities themselves did not know what they might have to hide. A trained archivist like myself was the last person they wanted prying, or, as they genuinely believed, spying. Willi escorted me back to the reception area. I thanked him for his help. He was naturally amused.

"You are very lucky. We combed the records when we first received your request. I am sure the personnel here are exceptionally thorough. We do not wish to be other than helpful but believe me when I tell you that it is exceptional to provide such help."

I thanked him again. At my request to visit the street where Hirschlich, or a relative, had lived, he shrugged. That would not be possible. I didn't enquire why. Willi wished to make the rest of my stay as pleasant as possible. I had one more day to spend in East Germany. He offered to take me to Berlin, to the East part of the city. I was surprised he did not know that my visa was for Leipzig only and I was specifically prohibited from visiting other places in East Germany. He did know. It would simply require a short visit to his office to have the visa amended and then tomorrow we would travel to Berlin in his car. His office was close to the records office in a converted nineteenth-century residential block. We entered through another dreary and uninviting entrance hall where Willi asked me to sit. Unlike the records building, the two receptionists, both men, wore military uniforms. When Willi entered, they stood up and saluted him. He returned the salute, momentarily dropping his urbane manner. He asked me for my passport and told me to wait while he disappeared into the building. I stood, as there was nowhere to sit, and tried to be inconspicuous, intimidated by the two men in uniform who kept me under close surveillance. It was not a place where civilians were to be found, even less westerners.

I did not have long to wait. Willi handed me back my passport and I looked at the page with the GDR visa. It had been amended by hand and then stamped and dated. We left the austere building and Willi resumed his gleeful manner.

"Tomorrow, Berlin. That will be good. However, I now have to address some other matters so will take you to the hotel where you will be given your lunch and dinner. It would be good if you were to stay at the hotel for the rest of the day. If you do leave, be assured, we will be with you, but better, better for me too, if you were to, let us say, write up your notes."

Laughing, he walked me to the hotel.

The trip to Berlin, like everything on my trip, had already been carefully arranged. I took my notebook and my camera. Willi frowned when I produced the camera and then laughed. That was how he dealt with me when I didn't quite fit into the plan that had been arranged for me. We set out early. The car was some sort of Soviet limo. When Willi fetched me from the hotel lobby, I realised, as I had done the day before when we visited his office, just how senior Willi was in the hierarchy. At such a young age already being groomed. I was flattered to be afforded so significant a minder. Willi's driver opened the door for me and then walked round to the other side to open the door for Willi. My single aim from this trip was to persuade Willi to let me take his photo. The drive took about four hours so we arrived around noon. Willi explained it was easier if we toured the city in the car as this would avoid drawing attention. We took in some sights. At the Pergamon Museum, I asked if I could take my photo. The driver remained in the car which was parked across the river from the façade of the museum. I posed the photo so that Willi is standing beside the car with the museum in the background. I didn't betray my surprise when Willi agreed to being photographed. He was this oddest of things: a man who relished breaking the rules in a place where rules were what mattered most entirely.

The lunch was good in a private dining room where the two of us sat alone. Willi spoke about growing up in Leipzig. His seniority and intelligence together with his youth and personality meant he could see things more objectively than some of his Party colleagues – his words. He had now no expectations. As coffee was being served a third man arrived, older than Willi, with greying hair.

"This is the Chief," Willi introduced him.

That was 1985 and no one, except I now think perhaps Willi, could see what would happen next. His no expectations hid a hope that even he hadn't dared express or imagine. I went back to Leipzig in 1991, after the fall of the wall. The place I had visited previously was now unimaginable. This was not because Leipzig the city had been transformed physically. It still then contrasted horribly with the affluence of the former West German cities I knew. What had vanished without trace was the sense of suspicion. Before paranoia was normal which in its own way banished sanity. Not only had that Leipzig vanished, disappeared without trace, it was also impossible to imagine that it had ever existed. So that Leipzig was more as a memory of a dream than of anything that could possibly really exist.

The tourist office was extremely helpful on my second visit. I had prepared before arriving with maps of Leipzig where I had identified the Hirschlich address from my previous visit. In the tourist office they supplied bus and tram maps and explained how I could buy tickets and which routes I would need to reach that part of the city. I explained I was looking for the street because it was where I believed one of my relatives had lived in the 30s. They responded positively to this explanation having looked at me a little quizzically when I first explained where I was going.

I followed their instructions and stepped off the tram at the designated stop late in the afternoon of an unseasonably hot April day. I had the map and looked for the street which meant I needed to cross the main road where the tram had dropped me. Across this busy arterial road, I could see some four or five storey concrete apartment buildings in the austere East German non-style. However, the area was lightened by a pleasant park that ran beside the main road and softened the hard edges of the apartment buildings. These had been laid out as an estate, so it was fortunate that the street with the Hirschlich address, Rosenthal Straße, had survived. However, it was clearly visible now, and unlike the estate, was curved with an older, original terrace of mansion type blocks along it.

Even here in what was clearly not a prosperous area the most obvious change were the cars. Along the street were parked a Mercedes and a BMW alongside the old Trabants that looked like mementos from a different country. I walked over the road, seeking gaps in the rush hour traffic as there was no pedestrian crossing. To reach Rosenthal Straße I needed to thread my way through the estate of apartment blocks. As I did so, in the early spring sunshine of the end of the day, reflecting off the neighbouring still bare branches of the park trees, I saw the women. They stood in the doorways to the apartments, in pairs or alone. In one apartment block there was a restaurant where a group of three women sat around an outdoor table drinking coffee. All the women smoked. Their dress was provocative and announced their trade. One of them left her partner and came up to me. I indicated I wasn't interested. It explained the quizzical looks at the Tourist Office. I was strangely shocked. I should not have been surprised but this was not what I expected to find. It contrasted with the nature of my own search, but also left me wondering about so many of the pictures in the Hirschlich collection. They celebrated the 20s, and the years before it, but were vividly underscored by a sense of the transparent poverty and despair of that time. It felt to me that I was revisiting a pre-war Germany, time trapped by the years of communism in the East and not yet captured by organised crime with all its trappings of capitalism and exploitation.

The woman went back to her partner where they stood and she lit a cigarette, nonchalantly, dismissing me with a small flick of her head. So many women, I guess it was early in their day. The men would come.

Rosenthal Straße retained its pre-war sense of domestic bourgeois propriety. It contrasted with the harshness of the estate I had just left. The buildings were terraced but attempted a little grandeur with a pillared portico for the main entrance. The number given was for an apartment in one of the buildings. The building was still there and the main entrance was unlocked so I entered. The actual apartment was on the second floor and I walked up the plain stone stairs. Despite the warmth of the April sunshine, in the stairwell it was still cold and dark now the light from the sun was fading. At Number 4, I rang the doorbell. There was no reply.

Now, reflecting back to that time, I cannot really recall what I had been expecting to happen or even why I had returned to Leipzig. No, I think the reason to go back to Leipzig was a curiosity about how it would seem after the 1985 visit. That was interesting. The unfreezing of a society after the hardship years of being part of the Soviet bloc. The hotel car park chock-a-block with Mercedes and BMWs with their bright West German number plates. The fact that people looked you in the eye and receptionists and officials introduced themselves by their name.

I stayed in the same hotel as before. The layout was unchanged but the cafeteria was open all day and had been remodelled into a coffee shop and more upmarket restaurant. The menu now offered pasta and pizza alongside some traditional dishes. I had the sauerkraut to remember Willi. I asked at the desk if they knew a man named Willi. I had brought the photo from 1985 with me. There was no flicker of recognition. When I went to the records office, which remained a municipal archive, the receptionist, who was obliging and helpful, also showed no sign of recognition when

I showed her the picture. This time I was given free rein in the records office, but the political changes had left them untidy and disrupted. In the free for all of freedom, the records were now open house and suffered from too much access. I could find no trace of the rows of archives of 30s planning and building permissions and licences Willi had shown me only six years before.

So all I have from my two trips to Leipzig are my handwritten note of the address in Rosenthal Straße for someone of the name of Hirschlich and my photo of Willi and his Soviet limo in front of the Pergamon museum in Berlin in former East Germany in 1985.

Willi

Catherine looked at the picture of Willi. She held it in front of her at the desk and then placed it back beside the notebook where Ben had recorded the address in Rosenthal Straße together with his handwritten note of his visit to Leipzig in 1985. In a separate set of notebooks she had found the reference to his second visit there. It was as good a place as any to start her search for Hirschlich. Her search for the missing art dealer within the Winter archivist's own records.

She thought of Ben in Leipzig in April because it was already now April in London and the imagined early, golden sunshine was in reality the sunshine across Bloomsbury Square where she walked that morning.

She had arranged to Skype Alain that morning. He was aware of her project. He considered it mad but interesting. She explained in emails that she would need to speak to him to verify certain facts, certain parts of Ben's story, of his history, that weren't completely clear from records. Alain was agreeable to this. He told Catherine he did not understand where her project was taking them, but he was willing to accompany her and help as far as he could. What he failed to understand was how she was happy to make up many facts, yet for some parts of the story she needed his verification. But then, he was an archivist not a historian.

The facts, Catherine explained, were the real things. Real places like Versur and real people like Willi.

Alain smiled on the screen when they spoke that April morning. His amusement, he explained, was in confirming that Willi was real when in reality Willi was about as fake – in Alain's opinion – as people came. He had been for a time a well-known part of the Winter Institute's machinery. When Catherine heard this, she understood that Willi did not disappear from the story. She was pleased as she liked her Willi and she liked the thread he provided from the Leipzig visit to the Winter Institute. What Alain did not know, until Catherine told him after reading in the archive, was that Willi was already known to Ben before he turned up at the Hirschlich Centre in Venice. Perhaps he had always been interested in the Winter Institute and that is why he had got alongside Ben in Leipzig. He may have had more of a motive than just spying on a spy.

Alain described the later version of Willi. He described him as someone who was open and not open about his past. He told people he had worked for the GDR government in a security role. It was nothing special, he claimed, just routine surveillance, reading letters, bugging telephones. Everyone was at some level spying on everyone else. Willi just did it professionally. Yet, Alain felt, this openness on Willi's part concealed things he didn't want known about his past. The visit by Ben to Leipzig and his meeting with Willi would be entirely consistent with Alain's perceived mistrust of not hearing the whole story. Willi was loud in telling whoever wanted to know about his GDR past; but there was more past there than he revealed. Alain surmised that Willi had his own reasons for seeking out the Winter Institute and for Ben's apparent compliance with suppressing knowledge of their earlier encounter.

Catherine was pleased. That was exactly what she needed to know. How was it that the archives could reveal so much, yet there were other facts she could only gather from Alain. Otherwise the records would be incomplete.

Catherine enjoyed her conversations with Alain. She enjoyed them more than her meetings with Ben. She wanted to ask Alain more about how he had got along with Ben. That would need to wait. Alain had invited her to Grenoble as soon as she was able. She was keen to go. It was charming any time of the year, he told her. In winter the beautiful snow and in summer the glorious sunshine. It was such a beautiful place to live. He pitied her stuck in London. She would go, she assured him, when Ben's book was finished and in the meantime she needed to get further stuck into his archive.

All that being said, in the lovely spell of April weather, Catherine had started potting again. Her Ben pots.

Versur 1980

I would live and work in Versur for over 30 years. Of course, when you first arrive in a place you do not imagine that, at least I certainly did not. I did not either go first to Versur. Nor did I know that 1980 would be quite such a turning point in my own life. 24 years old, I had no experience beyond my research and studies at UCL. Amazingly, looking back, I had yet formally to leave home. I was to leave the security of the tiny terraced house in Walworth, living with the two adoring and adulatory parents of me, their only child. First, I needed to secure the post I had been told about by my then academic supervisor Professor Evans. I held him in high regard. He was an unconventional figure whose disregard for the norms of respect and gravitas in the world of art history chimed with the times and worked for the media. However, it managed to irritate many of those who controlled the appointments and careers of academics like him. It was a surprise that he had been willing to supervise my doctorate. In fact he shared my passion for the detailed analysis of historic documents to argue for and against the impact, importance and aesthetic of individual artists rather than a more traditionally based approach. When he took me on as a junior lecturer after I had completed my PhD, I had learned to distinguish the showman he used for the media, and the relentless and austere academic discipline that won him, despite the irritation, respect and place. It was this that must have attracted Herr Winter. Herr Winter was certainly a traditionalist, but a traditionalist who believed he was not afraid of change or of the future. A traditionalist who believed he interpreted tradition as the need for constant reinvention and remoulding. Herr Winter was, although I do get ahead of myself, even more remarkably contrary than Professor Evans.

Professor Evans told me that the Winter Institute was looking for an archivist and he had recommended me for the post. If I was interested, I needed to get in touch with the Institute and an interview would be arranged. He was encouraging. Already he could see that changes being talked about for the English education system would make it a less appealing place. In any case, he remarked, there was no problem with returning at some point and nothing to stop me publishing under the aegis of the Winter Institute.

I acted without hesitation, telephoning the Institute and was invited to visit. I did not go to Versur. The invitation was to meet Herr Winter at their Grenoble property. The house was more like a hotel. It fronted a green square a short walk from the historic centre. The front door was reached by walking up a small but grand series of steps and I was greeted when I rang by a butler who escorted me upstairs to a first floor sitting room beautifully decorated in what I thought a Napoleon third style. Although elaborate and ornate, overstated I would say, it fitted perfectly the nineteenth-century town house, or something rather larger than a town house.

"A merchant's house," Herr Winter explained. He was waiting in the room standing by one of the full length windows that looked over the green and could be opened onto a small wrought iron balcony. He had asked me to describe the room to him. I had said Napoleon third and he had nodded. He asked me for an opinion, and again he nodded. This was the house his father had acquired after the war, the Great War, he explained, and was originally used for their business. The business had made them rich. He was quite open about their success as traders and then bankers that had created a significant fortune between the two wars. The proximity to Switzerland had proved essential to surviving the second war. They had removed the business there and all their assets.

All of this I knew. The Winter Institute is world renowned now as then. The UCL library provided a useful source of information with the Winter Bulletin, published since 1960, a frequent source for my own studies. There was a biography for Herr Winter senior and within this I had read the official history just as his son now told me.

Herr Winter appeared satisfied with my answers. He was shorter than I had expected. His stature rested in his commanding presence, with an assumed elegance of manner and assumption of importance. I was used to academic types, competitive, less concerned with the dignity of their appearance and manner as with the acerbity and incisiveness of their intelligence. I did not doubt also those qualities in Herr Winter. Yet he held them as a business man, as a person of commerce, rather than an arbiter of taste and knowledge. Crudely, I understood that he was the paymaster, we the performers.

We had still not shaken hands. I was standing just inside the door, he by the window questioning me, making, I am sure, a rapid and important assessment of his first impressions. If I had failed that test, would I have been politely excluded? Seeing him so many times later and working with him so closely I know the answer was yes. Still on this occasion, our first meeting in his beautiful family house – the merchant's house – I could not know this. So when he gracefully strolled across the floor and outstretched his hand, I was more than happy to shake it and accept at face value his welcome. He indicated for me to sit on one of the ornate and rather small sofas in the room. He then sat himself on its double at a right angle so that we were not directly facing each other. The butler re-entered and a coffee pot and cups and saucers placed on the table, equally ornately decorated, between the two sofas. We sat at right angles with another table and light forming the corner between the two abutting seats.

I recall this very vividly and with delight. However I may feel or have been made to feel by subsequent events, this remains a positive and defining moment in my life. As I examine my memory of these events, coloured as they are by this sense of opportunity, like a sun rising, a light being switched on, I don't really recall any further questions to me beyond those first two. How I would describe the room and then my opinion of it. This had always been described as a visit, never as an interview, and whether I am right to believe there were no further questions or I have simply forgotten them, they were not I think influential in my subsequent appointment. Instead of any kind of interrogation, Herr Winter spoke about the Institute, his family, how they wished to use their wealth for culture and the arts to contribute to peace in Europe.

I listened carefully. Herr Winter was more than impressive or inspiring. This was not the crass charisma of a political character. It was not a performance for the media. These were intensely held beliefs spoken by a man I believe genuinely dedicated to improving, well, let's be momentarily grandiose, the world. The authenticity of the person denied any need for cruder enthusiasm. You either bought into him, and to the Winter Institute, or you turned your back. He paused, sat back into the sofa, sipped the cup of black coffee. The space was for me to speak. I asked him about Versur.

He smiled. We would visit Versur together the next day. Versur was the dream of an eternal peace. Its architecture created that hope as reality when it opened in the aftermath of war in Europe. It was so influential that in the recent discussions for a new Musée des Beaux Arts here in Grenoble, President Mitterrand had contacted him directly to seek advice on the design. He would be involved in the shortlisting of the architects.

I realised that, whatever my politics – woefully undeveloped I now realise through a lack of interest – I was sat in touching distance of real power. It made me momentarily afraid and would later make me elated. Now, I am indifferent because power without being able to use it is a dead thing.

Now I remember there was a question. Yet it was not to assess me. It was to find out information. We were coming to the end of the time he had allocated for our first meeting, he explained. He wanted to know, but I did not need to decide there and then, whether on the basis of our first meeting whether, if it were offered, I would like to take the job. He assured me the terms would be very good. "You will not do better, if we decide to make the offer!" He smiled. "But that should not be the reason to take the job."

I said I would not have travelled so far if I was not serious about wanting the post. That, in fact, I felt very honoured and not a little overawed by our first meeting. That I could not in fact find any reason why I should not wish to grab this opportunity with both hands.

He was delighted and stood up to shake my hand again. That evening I was invited to return and dine with him and his father, Herr Winter senior, now in his seventies.

I left to return to my hotel. It was a small pension with a shared bathroom near to the station and a half hour walk from the house. Opposite the hotel was a quite noisy bar with an intimidating looking group of locals drinking. Nonetheless, I entered, took a seat and ordered in my indifferent French a glass of red wine. I was 24 and was trying to imagine myself in the world of the Institute. All those concerns of being 24. Saying and doing the rights thing, wearing the right clothes, arriving at the right time, not having enough money. I left the coins in the little steel tray and went back to my hotel room to wait for the dinner aware that I remained still in the seedier part of town. I had not yet crossed over, as I have come to think of it.

We would be visiting Versur in the morning. Herr Winter asked me if I wanted to be collected from my hotel. I said I was happy to walk over as I enjoyed the fresh air in the morning and could have some breakfast en route. Herr Winter was delighted. We were sitting at this moment in the same room in which he had entertained me earlier. I had been given a small glass of something quite sweet that I could not identify. I sipped it cautiously. It tasted very alcoholic and I was anxious not to get at all tipsy. I knew I lacked the sophistication that characterised Herr Winter's world. I knew that to pretend otherwise would be gauche. So I attempted to appear relaxed as a fish out of water might appear in the hope of being carefully restored to its original milieu. Yet I didn't want to return to my London way of life. Already I was hooked. So more like a fish being prepared for supper. The image did not sit well but now seems more apt than I might like to admit.

As we sipped our drinks Herr Winter spoke about the pride he felt in everything they had achieved in Versur. The wonderful buildings that hosted the Winter Institute itself. There were, he explained, daily tours for coach trips of visitors from all over the world. Architects, some of international renown, made their way to Versur to admire its modern style. Some of them had given him drawings they had made, in this way adding further to the Institute's great collection of twentieth-century art. It illustrated how the Institute worked organically to grow and instil art simply by its own existence.

He gestured for us to stand and I left my unfinished drink on the beautifully inlaid wooden occasional table. I followed him across the landing of the first floor to an intimate room laid out for dinner. There were three places and the butler was once again there pulling out a high backed dining chair where I was to sit. Herr Winter stood by his chair, his hand on its back and just as he had seated himself the door reopened to admit Herr Winter senior and I stood up again. The older man was, I had calculated from the UCL library biography, 73. His resemblance to his son was intense. I guessed this was in part because they had used the same barbers forever. Still the features were apparently carved out of the same marble. The older man showed no sign of age. If I had not known, I would have imagined him in his sixties, fifties even. Grey haired and with a determined edge in his manner suggesting someone fully engaged in an active working life.

This was in fact the case. Although Herr Winter was now the President of the Institute, his father remained as its Chair and, as I later found out, continued to have a great influence, especially in the commercial areas which, to be truthful, were of less interest to his son.

The butler helped the father into his chair. He patted the butler's arm with thanks as he sat. A sign of intimacy and showing just an element of that increased support he appreciated in his later years. We all sat down.

Herr Winter introduced me. I was surprised to hear myself described so positively. "A strongly recommended and most promising lecturer from University College London with an outstanding understanding of the background and provenance of twentieth-century European art."

It was peculiar to hear yourself described, as if at an awards ceremony, and to wonder if that were either true or possible. It was not my place to contradict. Instead I tried to look humble but I think probably just beamed with pleasure. The father was looking at me soberly. He was summing me up and it was necessary to speak.

I spoke admiringly of the beautiful house and of the most interesting discussion that afternoon with his son. I echoed Herr Winter's praise by telling his father how much I admired the Institute's art collection and even more its pioneering work to establish art and culture as the basis for peace for ever in Europe. The older man looked pleased at my references and my knowledge. My reading was paying off. I said that everyone had heard of the Winter Institute but not enough people recognised its bigger purpose over and above the great Hirschlich art collection in Venice.

"Tomorrow," Herr Winter said again this time for his father's benefit, "we visit Versur."

The small flicker of irritation on his father's face was momentary. Herr Winter saw that I had noticed it.

"Versur is not entirely to my father's liking."

The topic was not pursued as we were interrupted by the first course, served by the butler. The food was delicious; restaurant quality. The chef, Herr Winter told me, was from nearby Lyon. It struck me then, but I understood more later, as odd that the two men ate alone in their house. I knew both were married and their wives were alive. Were they eating in some other part of the house? This was more like a room in a hotel reserved for intimate private dining. There must be a proper dining room in the house for when the extended Winter family came together for celebrations.

I slept well although the hotel smelt and it was noisy. My travelling alarm clock woke me from a deep sleep. I had set it for five thirty as I wanted to be sure of using the shared bathroom ahead of the other guests. The bathroom was dirty and the toilet a disgrace. This early in the morning I had it to myself and was able to shower quickly and shave so that I only needed ten minutes. Then I realised I was far too early. It was still night time outside. The March day, as far as I could see in the dark, looked overcast and it had been raining. It was too early to look for breakfast. I had refused the hotel breakfast. The little breakfast room was no more than a badly fitted scullery.

In the cramped room I was able to write up my notes of the previous day's events. There was no table, so I sat on the one wooden chair with the notebook on my knee, the same notebook from which I am referring now and which gives me such confidence that my reflections are accurate. Let me share an extract.

The two Herr Winters are in appearance alike. However, the father appears to me much more of a businessman than his son. He responded positively to my comments about the Institute's purpose. I wonder if his interest in the Institute is more to do with its reputation. His son, having met him twice yesterday, does genuinely see the Institute as a way of putting the Winter fortune to a good end. He shares his father's vanity of the project, but it is part and parcel with the everyday fact of being wealthy, famous and powerful.

I am surprised more than thirty years later how accurate this is. What I did not record was my desire to join in with the wealth and splendour of the Institute. Nor did I write down and possibly even acknowledge to myself the willingness with which I was content to become as much a lackey as an employee of the Winters in pursuit of this, to me, noble aspiration. If had been capable of such complete honesty at that age, I would never have taken the job I then held for my entire working life. But I didn't know that then. So it is we do not know what we might have done and regretted or not.

I returned to the bar across from the seedy hotel for breakfast. It was excellent. The perfect preparation for my appointment at the Winter House. A car was parked outside and when I rang the bell Herr Winter answered already dressed for the journey and we immediately got into the car and left for Versur.

The day showed little sign of improvement. Overcast but not raining the light turned everything into different shades of grey. When we arrived in Versur, about an hour's drive – further than I had expected – from Grenoble, we parked by the church. This was the original centre of the village. Two streets ran at right angles from the church. Each street had the individual two storey chalet style houses of the area and the church was grey with a squat pre-revolutionary square tower. There was a modest chateau style building turned into a hotel at the end of one of the streets. Versur is situated in a valley formed by a quite small stream, and this ran behind the church away from the settlements. The area outside the village was and is densely wooded.

Turning our backs to the two simple streets of houses, we walked around the church and then across a small, rustic bridge over the stream which was still full from the winter rains. Although it was not raining, the overnight damp meant everything glistened and appeared covered with mosses and lichens. It should have been quite green, but the colours that day were subdued by the overcast sky. As we walked over the bridge, I remember that all I could see were trees and the undergrowth of the wood. The cleverness of Versur, of what the Institute had built there, was how it appeared gently and cleanly from among the tress. It seemed to me as I looked into the wood that the foliage began to take on the appearance of hard edges; corners, ledges, shelves which then turned out to be verandas and balconies. There were many levels. The hard edges turned into concrete. The concrete, unpainted or treated, was grey, especially grey the first time I saw it. Dug into a hillside or so it seemed because the wood stretched up around these concrete edifices.

I had strode out ahead of Herr Winter in my delight and excitement at visiting this place. As you stepped out of the wood, you stepped into the layered blocks and open squares of the Institute's buildings. These were laid out as a series of pavilions. The initial piazza that formed the first pavilion was built of a single storey elevated on narrow concrete stilts that created a cloister like effect and sense of space on all four sides leading the eye both straight ahead to the larger pavilions beyond and also on each side where a vista of further piazzas of more modest proportions beckoned. Realising I had left my host behind, I paused and waited for him to catch up. He did not treat my headlong rush into Versur as rudeness. I could see he was elated at my response to the beauty, originality and creativity of the place. He was metaphorically rubbing his hands with glee, a gleefulness that I only rarely saw in him. I took him at face value and shared his delight in the place his family had created and that I had, I believe, passed another important milestone in achieving the bond I now knew I undoubtedly wanted with this place.

Now having caught me up, he led the way. Undistracted by the piazzas to left and right – I later understood these were primarily living accommodation for staff, students, visitors, actors and the like – he took me into the next piazza. It was grander with the two storey buildings again elevated by the concrete stilts that created the spacious walkways beneath them. On the right hand side of the piazza as we entered, this pattern was broken by a blank, undecorated facade which had a ground floor entrance and a quasi-classical portico, simplified to its component parts. It gave the building an elegance that belied the need for grandeur. This was my first sight of the legendary English Speaking Theatre.

Around each piazza beside the covered walkway created by the elevated buildings ran a gravelled pathway about a metre wide allowing people to pass easily. Then in the centre of this piazza was an English garden, shrubs and herbaceous borders with small lawns and benches. It was an elegant play on the idea of the public park. So early in the year, I saw the carefully pruned rose bushes just beginning to sprout with this season's buds that would be filled with hybrid tea flowers later.

The shift from the old village and church of Versur through the wood and up the hill into the modernity of the Institute pleased me. There were few people about. I guessed it was a time at which people would be at work or in classes. Those people who did pass us were quick to greet Herr Winter who acknowledged them with the expectation of being known but not needing to know everyone he met. He continued to lead the way and walked through the pretend park, cutting the corner of the piazza, to the steps rising to the entrance of the English Speaking Theatre. He pushed open one of the glazed doors and we entered the foyer. There was a box office facing us and the single member of staff greeted us both with the warmth everyone so far had extended to Herr Winter. Herr Winter nodded in pleasant acknowledgement, explaining that he wished to give Mr Wilkins a tour of the theatre.

He unhooked the red plush rope that indicated the theatre was closed and we stepped inside. The theatre was silent and there were few lights on so it was quite dim. It took a moment to adjust our eyes to the gloom. I had expected the modern exterior to be reflected in the theatre's interior, not unlike the recently opened National Theatre in London. So I was amazed to see that instead the interior had been modelled on a typical London West End theatre. As there we were in the first circle, what I would call the dress circle, looking down past the balustrade to the stalls below. It was all gilt and red plush, the circle's balustrade curving round and above us another circle or balcony. I did clap my hands with my own sense of glee and the applause sounded well if hollow in the empty theatre.

Herr Winter stood behind me as I had stepped ahead while my eyes were adjusting to the gloom. Nonetheless, I could tell he was satisfied with my response. I heard him sit in one of the tip up red plush theatre seats. Turning to him, I sat across the small aisle in the corresponding row.

There were 365 seats, he explained, a silly, personal folly. It made the theatre intimate as it had been created as a perfect space for English plays, the plays his family had always adored. The manager was English and secured the services of various theatre companies through the year culminating in the one month tour in the summer by the Royal Shakespeare Company. Naturally the Institute subsidised the tickets as part of its educational aims. They were so popular, they needed to be allocated by ballot with 25% reserved for local schools, including, Versur College which was the Institute subsidised school for local children.

I listened yet did not need to pay too much attention as I had found this all out from my preparation for my interview. What I had failed to discover was the essence of Versur itself. Neither the wonder of the pastiche nineteenth-century theatre nor the total modernity of the Institute's campus were properly reflected in what I had read. I had stumbled across a wonderful secret that did not need to be a secret. Pre-empting my question Herr Winter told me the Institute had traditionally been shy of publicity. It had undertaken its work quietly, cultivating a level of obscurity that would avoid the need for publicity. Why, for example, advertise the productions and touring companies when there was already more demand for tickets than they could cope with?

We sat in the peaceful gloom of the empty theatre. Herr Winter was speaking very openly. Of course, just then, I mainly wanted to know how I was doing in terms of the job I now so badly wanted. Yet he continued in, I thought and hoped, a way that suggested I was already part of the set up at the Institute. His opinion on publicity was shifting. In fact the decision to appoint an archivist was part of that move. If the profile of the Institute was to be increased. For example, if they were to court publicity with all the implications that brought for the privacy of the family especially. It would be necessary to have in place excellent materials about the Institute and formalise and properly archive all the many records about how the Institute had achieved its extraordinary collection in pursuit of its artistic and altruistic aims. He spoke with great care and deliberation. He was a man who had given exacting consideration to the pros and cons, the possibilities and pitfalls. I saw a man now in his forties thinking about the future in a different way. It was a future that would not now always be his to create. His father's legacy was secure. We were visiting it. What did Herr Winter want his legacy to be? He paused before continuing to speak, the gloom highlighting his face as he leaned forward one of the low lights throwing his features into shadow.

"I find my empty, dark theatre an excellent place to think. When there are no players and you have to people the stage with your own imaginings. I have one more set of questions for you. Let me reassure you first that the job, following discussions with my father after your departure last night, is yours. You will be generously paid with free accommodation here in Versur. You will have great flexibility in how you deploy your time. The Institute would encourage you to travel as part of your efforts to understand and document the extent of both our holdings and their influence. You already have much of the expertise you need and what else is required we will pay for. If it is influential or important experts in whatever field, we will also make those introductions for you.

"Let me ask you in this creative space to imagine that there exists a whole spectrum of colours that we have never seen before. These are not simply variations on all the many colours and the words we have to describe them. I am asking you to imagine a completely different palette from these. Tell me what you see."

So I told him that what I saw was the future as imaginable, the unimaginable became imaginable and possible. I meant that beauty and goodness we think is impossible is very possible and only limited by what we think we know. I saw all these new colours and knew that what I saw was the infinite possibility of perfection and justice.

He reached across the aisle of the empty theatre and grasped my hand.

We lunched in the restaurant that served staff and visitors alike. It was a buffet arrangement and Herr Winter and I queued with everyone else to take our turn. I declined the offer of wine with the meal. I remember this lunch very precisely because it was there that my visit was interrupted by news about my mum's health. Later I found out my dad had tracked me down via Professor Evans. It was urgent. I should return as quickly as I could. For the first time I experienced the extent of the Winters' generosity. The car that had brought us from Grenoble and its driver were put at my disposal. We collected my things from the hotel there and stopped at the office while a ticket was booked on the phone for a flight from Paris. I was driven to the airport and so was able to be back in London that evening.

I took the tube straight from Heathrow to the Elephant and was walking the familiar route home. Home was empty as Dad would be with my mum. It was 8 pm and I wasn't sure when visiting stopped. Still the message had been very urgent – that is what the note handed to Herr Winter said – and so I went by bus to King's College Hospital where Mum was being treated.

Mum was in a side room and Dad looked inevitably tired and washed out sat beside her bed. He was in some amazement when I pitched up. He had only left his message with Professor Evans that morning and he belonged to a generation that still believed travel abroad was by pack animal. I was nonetheless much quicker than my normal route for trips to the Continent by rail and Channel ferry.

He stood up and shook me by the hand. The formality was unusual and unnerving. I looked at him with the unvoiced question about Mum and he looked at the ground then hugged me. That was also unusual. As I describe us it is like watching us in a film. Then I went out to find another chair as there was only one in the room.

You forget how inadequate and hopeless hospital care was at that time. The under maintained Victorian hospital buildings, the worn floors and the sense of hopelessness in the staff. Hopeless because there was no money and hopeless because then there was so little that could be done in the face of illnesses like my mum's. She must have known for a while she had been ill. So the doctors told us. It meant that the time between her diagnosis and death was quite short, just seven days. She was in a coma or unconscious for a large part of it. The doctors told us it would have made little difference if they had diagnosed her sooner. The course of the disease was what it was. The seven days were difficult. At the start of that week I went back to work. Professor Evans was keen to know more about the Winter Institute. I was genuinely enthusiastic about the Institute, Herr Winter and especially Versur. I was also clear in my thanks to my Professor for making the link. He in turn was optimistic that we could create some academic links between UCL and the Institute. I explained the basis of my role and sought his advice on how to extend my archival skills.

As the week went past and my mum weakened and lapsed more frequently into unconsciousness, I asked and was granted the leave I needed to be with my dad. He was distraught and for the first time I experienced that adult feeling of needing to parent your own parents. This for me meant taking food to my dad as he sat in the hospital, then sitting with him. There was not much to talk about. The doctors visited less and the nurses more. There was a discussion about Mum coming home; 'to die' was the implied suggestion. As it happened Mum's death pre-empted that plan and then it was me and my dad in the house in Walworth organising the funeral with a local funeral director. One of the men working there had been at school with my dad and I remember thinking how there remained a community of sorts and hoping it would help my dad when I returned to Versur.

The sense of letting him down accompanied a deeper feeling of loss. It was the loss of place, of where I had grown up and where I had chosen to continue to live through early adulthood. The loss was of course also for my mum. The timing was good and awful. Maybe it was good because it was awful. You think back and see yourself living through these events. My dad would continue to live in the house alone until just a few years ago now.

Using the memory of that sense of loss: my mum, home, Walworth, I try to imagine how I was then when I accepted the job at the Institute as the Winter Archivist. The excitement and expectation are embedded in that loss and grow out of it and above it. The entire set of events, both the events themselves and the feelings I remember are exceptionally and solely two dimensional. Like a child's drawing they lack the third dimension of depth, of reflection.

When I thought then about Herr Winter, any reflective ability did not function or even exist. It would be incorrect to say that I was taken in. There was no deliberate attempt to pull the wool over my eyes. True, I was dazzled – by the wealth, the generosity, the architecture, the ambition, the power. I wanted to be dazzled and I wanted to believe in the completeness of it, like believing in the fictional world of a fairy tale. So perhaps I was enchanted. I think that is how I can best describe my state of mind and emotions when I arrived in Versur. Yet if there was a magic spell that created my state of enchantment, it endured a long time and still, in my heart, I want it to endure now. The spell never ended with a simple snap. Instead I slowly woke, or my sense of scepticism slowly eroded the gentle slumber of my enchantment and my enchanted world.

1980 my mother has died and I leave my dad living by himself in the family home in Walworth and set myself up in Versur in my new job as the Winter Archivist. I lived in the first piazza to the right of the entrance pavilion. This was the Japanese pavilion with a beautifully maintained Japanese stone garden at its centre and two trees, an acer and a slender cherry. My new home where I would live for so many years until my retirement. My retirement, so called, is a bitter thought at such a tranquil moment of my life to date. Good beginnings may be never lead to good endings and that ending was even worse than I experienced it at the time.

So if I had been the sceptic then that I later became where should I have been casting my gaze. I know the answer now, of course. Yet the clue was prominent. It is right under my nose.

Herr Winter had been his usual generous and perfect self when I had to inform him of the sad news of my mum's death. He conveyed his sincere condolences. The Institute sent a modest and perfect wreath to the funeral. That certainly impressed my dad. It was a typically kind gesture. He also was keen for me to start as soon as was feasible. He did not want to put me under any pressure but hoped I would be able to take up the post in the spring and at least before the summer. This worked too for UCL and I was released by my Professor not least in the hope of establishing the much desired academic link with the Institute. The focus of my work, over and above formalising the archive of the family and the Institute, was to be what had come to be known as the Hirschlich Collection. This superb collection of over 50 twentieth-century canvases and drawings from before the war was held by the Institute in gift from the art dealer Hirschlich. Herr Winter was, however, deeply unhappy that there was so little documentation on the Hirschlich provenance. It would be a primary part of my job to establish that provenance more securely than the scanty family records. Even Herr Winter Senior who had received the collection had never himself personally met Hirschlich who had disappeared in the Germany of the thirties before the Winters themselves, with their collections, had evacuated to Switzerland at the start of the fighting.

The good news was that the Hirschlich Collection was then exhibited in Venice at the Winter's former merchant house on La Giudecca.

Herr Winter

When Catherine met Herr Winter for the first time it was at Versur. She was disappointed by both. Herr Winter was not the urbane, cosmopolitan connoisseur she had imagined and Versur had become an overgrown, concrete campus. She instantly considered rewriting entirely her account of Ben's life. Before she could consider her options further, she recalled that Herr Winter had already received her original version with no explanation as to its authorship. She had left this deliberately vague. Herr Winter introduced himself. He was accompanied by a middle aged woman. There was no mention of the ghost writer, no mention of Ben's bequest. This, she learned, was Friederike, his only daughter and now the Chief Executive of the Winter Institute. It was morning and it was summer. In a week's time the statue of Herr Winter's father – the man Ben always referred to as Herr Winter senior – would be unveiled. Herr Winter had invited her to this event on receiving Ben's autobiographic account of his time at the Institute. The book she had authored on his behalf. Tea was served in the smallish office where they were meeting. It was unexpectedly business like. Catherine perched on a swivel chair with wheels that had been brought in from a neighbouring office when she had arrived.

Perhaps Catherine was being unfairly judgemental of Versur and the Winters, father and daughter. There was, she admitted as she sipped her too weak tea, a kind of urbanity about them. As for the place, what little she had seen of it did not inspire her in the way she had imagined Ben to be inspired when he had first seen it all that time before. She meant to ask Herr Winter a number of questions. He was also perched, this time on the edge of the desk behind which his daughter was seated. Catherine assumed this to be her office. Almost instantly she was corrected by Friederike. Friederike was apologising that because of the upheaval in a week's time with the statue unveiling, this office was the only available space for them to meet. It had in fact originally been Ben's office when he had worked here as the Winter Archivist. Friederike smiled, believing this would be seen by Catherine as a nice gesture.

Nice was the word that featured most in Catherine's mind. The nice Herr Winter and his nice daughter Friederike in their nice, cosy office where Ben had worked. Here he had sifted through the jumbled records of the Winters establishing how they had moved from merchants to philanthropists and patrons of the arts. Here he had tried to solve the Hirschlich problem.

Herr Winter was speaking now. It seemed Catherine was to have a number of explanations. Not only was Versur in uproar in preparation for the unveiling. A number of famous people she was made to understand would be arriving including the French President who would be landing in a helicopter quite close. They were delighted she had accepted the invitation. The book she had sent, Ben's book, was something they had read with interest. Catherine noted that father and daughter acted in unison, spoke in the singular. They wished to speak with her about it. However, more explanations, not immediately. Would it be possible for a longer meeting to speak about its contents after the unveiling, perhaps a few days afterwards when especially Herr Winter had had the opportunity to rest a little, to recover. Really for both of them to recover.

She found herself nodding in agreement. At the same time she would need to extend her booking at the hotel in Grenoble. She hoped she would be able to stay in the same place as it was convenient for the station and for Alain who lived near the older part of the city. It was a busy time of the year, although Alain had said Grenoble was more busy during the skiing season than in the summer. Catherine had been surprised by how much she liked the place itself. It much more closely resembled where she imagined Ben had first met Herr Winter and been offered his job at the Institute. This inspired her to ask if the meeting after the unveiling could take place in Grenoble. A date and time were agreed at the Winter residence there.

They apologised that the hotel they recommended to guests in Versur was fully booked. It usually was, they smiled, but especially because of the unveiling. In fact, the Institute had booked the whole hotel which only had six rooms for their most valued guests. Their apology was quite unnecessary. Friederike asked her where she was staying. She picked up the telephone on the desk. She spoke rapidly in French. Putting down the phone, Herr Winter explained they would arrange her extended stay and naturally, the Institute would be pleased to pay for this as their guest.

Catherine, taken aback, thanked them. She was too effusive and the Winters held up their hands, palms facing her. They were delighted to help. Not only was she a great friend and confident of their much missed archivist, she was herself an artist for whom the Institute had the greatest regard and wished to support as part of its mission.

Bloomsbury 1986

One of the pleasures of working for the Winter Institute were my regular trips to Venice. Here the Hirschlich Centre had been established in the mid-50s to house the Hirschlich Collection. I sat in Herr Winter's office at Versur. The following year, scheduled for May 1995, the completely modernised, extended and redesigned Hirschlich Centre would reopen after being closed for the best part of two years. Herr Winter wanted me to update him with the latest version of my guide to the Hirschlich Collection. I knew he felt an anxiety that my work on the provenance of the collection was making little headway. However, he was too polite or maybe just circumspect to speak directly of the matter.

    Claude was away skiing. I did not go with him on these trips. He enjoyed the sport so much. I was a drag on that enjoyment as I skied so badly and with such little enthusiasm. He was better with a group of skiers as talented as he was. The previous summer season, summer 1993, had been his greatest success to date as Director of the English Speaking Theatre. In a daring move that initially proved controversial with Herr Winter, a French production of Tartuffe was mounted alongside Wycherley's the Country Wife. A single company of bilingual actors had been recruited to play both plays in rep, the first in French and the second in English. The stars from the same company had also appeared in the classic absurdist French play, Cardinal Richelieu. I remember that Herr Winter's doubts, that were more or less a dislike of doing a French play in the sacred English Speaking Theatre, had been overcome by the insistence of his daughter Friederike who doted on Claude. Before she had gone away to study at university and then to business school, she had spent all of her teenage holidays working with the successive companies in each summer season. She adored Claude as an artistic genius. So did I. He was. The season had been a spectacular triumph attracting attention from critics not only in Europe but also in New York. Cardinal Richelieu had transferred to off Broadway and the season had sparked renewed interest in its veteran author culminating in a season of revivals in Paris.

Of course I remember the date. It was January 15 1994. Herr Winter sat holding the draft of the pamphlet I was working on describing the new Hirschlich Centre. Instead of paying attention to his concerns about the failure to identify Hirschlich in Leipzig or Berlin before the war, I was thinking about Claude, about the success of the previous year's season, of the work he had lined up in London in the spring that would allow us once again to live together freely in the flat in Bloomsbury. We were interrupted by Herr Winter's assistant. He spoke quietly to Herr Winter who asked me to wait while he excused himself from the room. I took no particular notice. It was not especially unusual. I tended to forget that my work as archivist was of limited importance in the grander scheme of the Institute's undertakings. For example, I amused myself by thinking, Claude's triumphs on behalf of the English Speaking Theatre. Now that really did put the Winter Institute on the map. Same as with the Hirschlich Centre and the reopening a year hence.

So when Herr Winter returned I was completely unprepared that the reason for the interruption had to do with me.

Claude was in a coma. There had been a skiing accident. He had hit his head. He had been badly injured. I tried to understand. I was being told things. It was difficult to understand all these different facts. I needed to know how badly he had been injured. No one could tell me. That is how I knew he was very badly injured indeed. Herr Winter immediately organised his car and driver to take me to Switzerland to the hospital where Claude was being treated. When we arrived later the same day, then I found out he was not in a coma, he had died. It was still January 15 1994, there would be no more Claude summer seasons at the English Speaking Theatre.

Bloomsbury means for me art and food. The flat we bought there was a refuge. In Bloomsbury for the first time I discovered London as a place of pleasure. The pleasure was afforded by the love of Claude. Yet it persisted even until the present day. It is where I have chosen, after my time as the Winter Archivist, to live.

Claude and I were breakfasting the morning after we had been to see *The Normal Heart* at the Royal Court. That had been a sobering evening for two youngish gay men. For Claude more than me. He spoke frankly of his own problems as a gay boy growing up in Switzerland. Unlike me he had succeeded in establishing a place for his gayness in the world of theatre. Now that made him edgy. We knew so little.

Breakfast was poached eggs on toast for me and bacon and eggs for Claude. There was a small family owned café in, I think, Museum Street that was open all hours. Two Maltese men ran the place as an Italian version of a British greasy spoon. The breakfasts were especially good. Also for lunch or dinner the lasagne, the Caprese salad or the spaghetti meatballs. These are the cafés now largely lost from London replaced by the chains of coffee houses which, in some way, replicate them. Even the people are a little the same. Claude and I never questioned how two fat Maltese men posing as Italians came to be running an apparently family owned Italian café in Museum Street. I cannot even remember when it closed. One time, I noticed walking past that it was no longer there and bizarrely to my mind, had been replaced by a dry cleaners itself long since gone.

We were early and had the place to ourselves. Claude had a series of pre-rehearsal meetings with his production team at the Opera House and needed to be there by 8am. The Maltese were being charming and amusing. I drank tea and Claude drank coffee and the refills were rapid and endless. We had stayed up a little at the flat after returning from the play. We were drinking a good Côtes du Rhône and as I say, sober and sombre.

Claude knew people infected and at the Opera House there had been a collection for someone terminal. It was the fear of not knowing and we knew it was this.

I knew this morning Claude wished to break this dark mood. He was making some effort to be bright. He genuinely looked forward to the rehearsals. This was his first opera commission. We both knew that this was in large part because of the Winter Institute. Naturally, the Winter Institute was sponsoring the production. While Herr Winter insisted that there was no connection to Claude's appointment as its director, none of us could ever be sure. It was true that Claude had been offered the chance before he was appointed as Director of the English Speaking Theatre. Still, with Herr Winter you could never be sure.

Claude was laughing as he speared his bacon and egg together with some fried bread. I wondered at how easily he embraced some parts of British culture while being appalled by things like pubs. He had, after a week of preparation and then a week of rehearsal, won his argument. *Eugene Onegin* was going to be staged as full blown romantic love story, no holds barred. Tchaikovsky would have understood AIDS, but that didn't mean you needed to turn a great operatic spectacle into some kind of gay/AIDS ritual of discrimination and ignorance. Even as he said this, I could imagine the trendies wanting Claude to show his mettle with a full throttled modern production that shocked the traditionalists. Too bad. What they had failed to understand was that Claude was underneath it all a traditionalist, a purist. In a time when conceptual versions of the great stage works were in vogue, he made his name by an unashamed adherence to what he found in the pieces themselves. He wished to strip them back to something essential. He continued to amuse himself and me. Whatever people may wish to think to the contrary, *Eugene Onegin* remains a complete work of escapism for a bourgeois audience whose only difference from when it was written is being less elegantly attired. This was what Herr Winter understood about becoming Claude's patron.

Claude paid for breakfast, over-tipping as usual to the gratification of the ever friendly Maltese. He grabbed his large shoulder bag and we left each other outside as he headed off to Covent Garden. We would meet later for lunch. We had discovered the odd pleasure of eating stale smoked salmon sandwiches left over from the previous night's performance as our lunchtime staple. Claude preferred to eat with me as it excused him from having to spend the time with the company or production team.

I made my way back to the flat. It was too early still to go to the reading room at the British Museum where I was continuing my enquiries into the Hirschlich Collection. There was only a limited source of material in the UK. I mainly just enjoyed the access a reader's card gave me to the reading room where I could in fact work on the papers most of which I brought into the building with me. I had linked to the Imperial War Museum and the Jewish Museum as well as the Public Records Office. There appeared to be no reference to any Hirschlich in any of these sources. This primarily led me to rule out any possible appearance of Hirschlich or any members of his family in the UK as, for example, a refugee from the Nazis. This was consistent with the very little I had found to date about Hirschlich and pointed to the unproven conclusion that he had perished in Germany.

I cleared up the wine glasses from the previous night's discussion. I realised we had been too disturbed by the contents of the play to comment on just how fine it was and how superb the acting. Now it stands rightly as a step of enlightenment; but then, on the threshold of enlightenment, we did still remain if not ignorant in doubt.

I spent only half an hour in the reading room. It was not crowded as I entered at the opening time but was beginning to fill up. I did not want to take up a place unnecessarily.

Collecting my papers, not many, in the folder *Hirschlich in London/UK?* I went out of the back entrance and made for Russell Square. The day was bright but not really warm enough yet to sit on one of the benches so I made for the café in the corner near the tube station. I was thinking I might take the tube down to Covent Garden although Claude, if he found out, would criticise me for being so lazy not to walk. I would explain to him that part of the charm for me was using the lifts at both stations and admiring the stations themselves. He would throw up his hands and look at me aghast. He understood but really did believe this was crazy English behaviour.

With Herr Winter I felt I had a privileged relationship. After my mum's death, it had proved personally beneficial to locate immediately to my beautiful Versur and this had bonded me to the Institute in a unique way. Herr Winter knew my personal circumstance as he had witnessed it first-hand. This too, I felt, created a unique bond. Herr Winter often invited me to sit in meetings with him that were really unrelated to my work. His excuse was that by listening in, so to speak, to the way in which the Institute conducted its business, I would gain a better understanding. The meetings were usually conducted in English, occasionally in French or even German. I had been working to recover the two languages, which I had studied at school, but still found it hard to keep up with what was being said. A greater benefit was in accessing the documents in the archive in these languages.

One of these meetings was, Herr Winter told me in advance, on a more personal matter. It was with a senior partner from an accounting firm based in Zurich. There was no immediate business connection between Winter and the firm. However, the partner was an acquaintance of Herr Winter in the way these wealthy individuals always were. It was not explained why I was present but quickly became apparent. Starting in German, Herr Winter asked if his acquaintance would mind shifting to English on my account. I apologised for the need for this, but it was waved away.

The man explained that a recent trainee with the firm, an excellent member of the staff who had in fact recently qualified as an accountant with excellent marks, had made a bad and irrevocable mistake. He had publicly announced that he was a gay man. This meant that he would have to leave the firm. Herr Winter's help was being sought to find him a suitable alternative future as there was no ill will felt towards him, quite the reverse. There was just the regret that he had made such a bad mistake as to acknowledge he was gay. This was simply not possible for any employee in the firm.

It was never stated why I was there although it was quite clear to all three of us that I was needed. Perhaps I was considered not so foolish as publicly to state I was gay. Perhaps, because I worked in the institute with its artistic and cultural credentials, it meant it did not matter quite so much.

Peter, that was his name, and I met up after the meeting. I didn't ask Claude along. I would tell him later. He would be angry at the treatment Peter had received. My approach was to give up on the indignation and do something practical for the man. We met in the Institute's restaurant. It was a canteen really, but Herr Winter insisted on referring to it as a restaurant. I had immediately been impressed that a work canteen served wine at lunch and dinner. The restaurant was popular and always busy. It was a self-service affair. I usually ate the healthy salads in different varieties that were weighed at the checkout. Each day cooks would prepare the special of the day in front of you if you preferred something hot. The Institute prided itself on its range of international cuisine. The food was of a high quality, and in line with the Institute's concern for its workers, subsidised.

Peter only wanted a coffee. I encouraged him to have something more substantial as it was lunchtime and I wanted at least to pay as he had lost his job. I asked him what he intended to do and clearly he had no idea. He was upset. I perceived he was more embarrassed at having been humiliated by being discussed in his absence in our previous meeting. He had been asked to wait outside. What about a job, I encouraged him. He shook his head. We both sipped our coffees. Was he sure I could not get him something for lunch. To my surprise he relented and we returned to the self-service counters. He opted for the chicken chasseur with plenty of vegetables including a generous helping of the pommes dauphinoise. I opted for my usual medley of salads and some cheese. We waited our turn in the queue as the restaurant had become busier since our earlier cup of coffee. We took our plates to our existing places where we had left our coats. I poured two glasses of tap water from the jug on the table.

It was clear to me from Herr Winter's manner that my role was to help Peter. Essentially this meant finding him a job. We discussed his interests. It turned out that he was a great admirer of the Institute. He strongly believed in its aim of furthering culture. We did not discuss sexuality. I have no idea whether he intuited mine, and if he did what he made of that. Had the Institute produced its 'gay' man to give him a helping hand? That was, I think, pretty much the crass truth of it.

I took his details before we parted so that I could contact him. I also had his permission to seek alternative employment for him. He clearly would like a job at Versur. I couldn't guarantee that, so we also agreed to look at possible openings in Zurich. His previous boss had assured us all in the meeting that Peter would receive excellent references excluding any mention of his sexuality. The worse offence appeared his naivety in stating it openly.

I returned to my office. Office is a little overstating what was in fact a rather small room with a desk and chair for me. There wasn't really room for another chair, partly because I needed a table on which I could sort out the various documents and records that I was steadily cataloguing as the Winter Archive. The office was the entrance to the large shelved area, with no external light, in which the Archive was slowly being stored in a primarily chronological arrangement around the key themes of the Institute's history and business. I was using a card index system to cross catalogue the numerically ordered records.

The office and archive were in the main administrative part of Versur and the Directors' offices ran along one side of the corridor on the floor above. This included Herr Winter's corner office from which he could see out into the Versur campus as well as to the wood leading back to the original village and church. You entered this office through his secretary's adjacent office – itself larger than mine. It had never occurred to me to be bothered about my tiny office; not until Claude expressed his disbelief that I could be treated less well than Herr Winter's secretary. I smiled and remained calm. From the start, I have been clear about my relative importance. Herr Winter's secretary was in a higher league from me.

Nonetheless, as I have explained, I enjoyed a close personal relationship with Herr Winter and this allowed me to see him without requiring the usual formality of an appointment. It gave me an inside track for which his secretary was clearly briefed and encouraged. I sensed there were few colleagues with whom Herr Winter enjoyed a personal closeness. This was not deliberate on his part. I found him always to be charming. Unlike Claude who found conversations with Herr Winter forced and difficult, I allowed myself to relax into the grip of his dominant view to the extent that I enhanced his sense of his own significance. Herr Winter also perhaps experienced conversations with Claude as difficult. Claude was at Versur because of his artistic credentials. I was there as someone with a more straightforward job to do.

So after lunching with Peter and seeing him off in an Institute car to Lyon station for his return journey to Zurich I nipped in to see if Herr Winter had a moment. He was free and as always gracious. He wanted to know what I thought of our young visitor and expressed cautious regret over Peter's indiscretions at his work place. I told him we had lunched together and he nodded with approval. Then I made a mistake. I was too enthusiastic when I asked Herr Winter if it would not be possible for Peter to work at Versur, especially given his admiration for the Institute. That would not be possible. Herr Winter shook his head and waited. I was momentarily nonplussed. I thought of Claude. Could we ask the Director of the English Speaking Theatre if he had any contacts in the theatre world in Zurich. Herr Winter stood to signal the end of informal chat. That was an excellent suggestion, he acknowledged. He really had no one he could rely on more than his Archivist.

Lovely Claude ranted. He was furious. Furious at Peter's treatment. First his dismissal, then his humiliation being carted off here to be helped. He was furious with me for collaborating. He was furious that he, Claude, and his contacts had been offered as a solution. He wanted to resign. He felt I was weak and useless and threatened to end our relationship. On that he quickly relented. He forgave me. He could be histrionic. I apologised. I apologised from my heart as I felt as he did but knew better than to express it. I asked him to reconsider helping Peter. It was necessary. Claude could behave in certain ways because of his artistic talent. For most gay men, and that included me, this was not an option. Not then. Claude railed and then relented. Peter was found a job in the accounts department of a film and television company in Zurich. I hoped he forgave my weak and useless surrender to Herr Winter and the Institute.

That was the 80s. That is why we bought the Bloomsbury flat. Claude stayed at Versur. His compromise was to be circumspect in our relationship – an open but unacknowledged secret – in Versur. However, Bloomsbury now became where our hearts could bloom and our love thrive. To keep Claude, Herr Winter needed to allow me the space to live part of the year in Bloomsbury. To keep Claude he needed to share me.

In part Claude and I chose Bloomsbury because of the Opera House commission. The spring of 1986 was the first time we had lived in our flat there. We acquired it at the end of the previous summer. That summer was the first of the full seasons directed by Claude at the English Speaking Theatre. His impact had been enormous. It had catapulted the theatre to international acclaim, and with it the Winter Institute. It began the establishment of the Winter Institute as one of the most notable arts and cultural foundations in Europe. A reputation that would be finally confirmed when the Hirschlich Centre reopened in Venice in 1995.

A week on and rehearsals were on track. Claude was thoughtful and energetic during these periods of intense creativity. He combined, how I loved him for it, the ability to reflect intellectually while building something with the physical energy of a sculptor in marble. He said he never knew if it was good or not. He wasn't terrified of failure. He acknowledged that failure created the precipice for success – artistic success. His energy in the rehearsal period was countered by a magical self-erasure as soon as the production was finished. I used to argue with him. How can it be finished? All my experiences in the theatre were of fluid, moving, changing, breathing things – especially the great experiences. He was patient with me. That is because the productions are living, but they are finished in terms of their birth. Their die is cast. So they are finished. The costumes do not change. The sets do not change. The cuts to the score and libretto remain. The indulgences and retrenchments to the original remain.

Our pre-rehearsal breakfasts were now over. Claude needed to be at the rehearsal space from early until late. He was pleased to report that one of the singers – an internationally renowned soprano playing Tatyana who had only arrived this week and would be away again for the week immediately before opening night – she had been speaking to the conductor. The maestro, she told Claude as she patronised him with a small piece of artistic gossip, was an admirer. More, he had been extremely pleased by the approach Claude was adopting. A traditional, the term to which he reduced Claude's artistic contribution, production would suit his personal interpretation and encourage the orchestra and the singers.

Claude laughed at this. He admired both the singer and conductor because they were artistic geniuses of huge reputation. He had no difficulty working with them but did not feel so much part of them as a contributor in his own terms to creating the living production – the production that would not change.

We continued to meet for lunch. Today there were no sandwiches as there had been no performance the previous evening. The canteen produced soup. "Nip and nip soup," I explained to Claude. He was puzzled by this, but nonetheless ate it with good grace. He fetched an extra roll. He needed more energy for the afternoon.

The early morning he explained over the rather dismal lunch had been spent in St James Park with the costume designer who needed a long conversation about how to match Claude's ideas. She had been holding out for Dior style post war costumes which were now ridiculously at odds with the flamboyantly romantic period nature of the piece. Although she had known this for some time, she had continued to hold on to some notion of modernity and alienation. The set designer contrariwise was revelling in Claude's 'traditional' approach and only arguing over the paucity of the budget.

They walked in the earlier part of the morning with an increasing number of commuters hurrying past them on the footpath by the end of the lake nearest Whitehall. They were making progress, Claude had felt. Yvonne, the designer's name, would have to give way. It was just about how she could do so with good grace and the more important part, be relied on to produce the spectacular costumes Claude desired. As she spoke at length, mainly about her marriage and desire for children soon, they watched an army officer walking towards the park from Horse Guards. He crossed the road. He was middle aged and dressed in a formal uniform. Watching him, Claude was imagining an argument based on how the formality of uniforms could somehow capture Yvonne's underlying argument for style and regimented fashion in her proposed Dior look.

Just behind the officer they could see a dog, a retriever perhaps but clearly a pedigree. The officer walked with an air of complete authority. He was someone in charge, confident. Someone you did not take on. He was obviously walking his dog in the park. Walking as if he owned it.

Claude was animated telling me this story. With his second roll he had fetched some pate and salad. He stopped eating while he spoke. At the point, he told me, he was about to try the line about the formality of the officer's uniform, the dog scampered past them both across the path towards the lake. They watched it as it leaped over the small fence between the grass and the lake and sank its teeth into one of the tiny ducklings that had been following their parents towards the water. It was, Claude said, truly horrifying. He was laughing and apologised because although it was funny, it was also gut churning.

Yvonne had failed to see anything amusing about this and ran over to the officer and started berating him for allowing his dog to savage the duckling. She became tearful. The officer, who held the dog's lead in his hand, rapidly recovered the animal and leashed it. He was put out. He had a distressed woman and his dog had savaged one of Her Majesty's ducklings. This was not part of his usual experience.

Now Claude was seriously laughing. The officer, whose name turned out to be Richard, was seriously apologising. He immediately offered a cup of tea in Horse Guards and accepted without hesitation that he was in the wrong. He accepted blame in the way you do when you know it will be without consequence. It was no less sincere for that. They accepted tea. It was served in the officers mess in fine china. Ceylon, Richard commented, Nurwara Eliya.

I asked Claude whether Yvonne had come over to his way of thinking about the costumes. The brigadier, it turned out, was a fan of the opera. His mortification increased accordingly when he learned he had Claude and Yvonne in his mess. Yvonne, Claude acceded, had been charmed to the extent that she invited Richard and his wife to the first night as her guests. She also casually told Claude that she had rethought the costumes. They needed to be much more aligned to the spirit of the production. Much more regimented.

Claude was in a hurry to get back to his rehearsals. His Tatyana would only now be able to rehearse for the next two days before other engagements required her to fly to Barcelona. Opera was a pain, he admitted. Those lunches were so pleasurable. Claude enjoyed that Bloomsbury summer. The summer the duckling was eaten by the brigadier's dog in St James Park. One of Her Majesty's ducklings, according to the brigadier.

As he got up from the table I said I would just be a few moments to finish my coffee.

"By the way," he said, "I've invited Peter to the first night as well. I wonder what Peter will make of the brigadier."

We laughed.

I didn't immediately know who Claude meant by Peter. I was still amused by his duckling anecdote. "Pity and terror," he had said to the brigadier, who winced. Also I was glad the production appeared so on track. Here backstage at Covent Garden I did not want to jinx it, but knew I would not, could not. There was always that certainty with Claude. He would be criticised, we knew, for playing it safe, for always being mainstream. Yet I saw the opposite. I saw the danger and risk of not going for the controversial, the revolutionary, as some form of creative genius. That was Claude's precipice; a precipice of the ordinary.

I walked to St James Park. No evidence there of the savagery of the morning. I wondered if the busy commuters had noticed. Whether they would be telling their horrified families over dinner the shocking events that had taken place. We had been away from Versur for nearly five weeks now. I had taken the time as leave. However, Herr Winter had been generous in suggesting a discretionary extra three weeks for the London research that was in large part pointless. I didn't feel any sense of entitlement to this extra holiday but I also felt no sense of abusing my employer. It was a relationship based first on competence, and now increasingly on trust and friendship. I did not count Herr Winter as a friend. That would be presumptuous. Instead, I felt I was a friend of the family, of the Institute, a part of an extended family.

The spring weather was becoming warmer and I decided to take the bus down to the Old Kent Road to drop in on my dad. I had seen him when we first came over. Then Claude and I had met him for a slightly strained dinner which I agreed with Claude we would not repeat. Claude was charming and presented as the great director, overawing my dad. Claude and I agreed that there would be no acknowledgement of our sexual relationship. I certainly hadn't come out at home. Claude was irritated but went along with the limits I knew existed then for my family. There was a desultory discussion of musicals, which my mum had liked and Claude definitely didn't. I hope my dad was none the wiser when we put him in a taxi we paid for back home. The expense of the whole evening left him out of his depth.

I should have been back to see him sooner than this but had made myself excuses and not done that. The sunshine and better weather made it a more attractive proposition. When I arrived unexpectedly he was very pleased to see me. He put the kettle on and we ate chocolate digestive biscuits, his personal treat I thought, and talked about Mum. He told me he had enjoyed the dinner with Claude. That he wasn't used to spending time with such important people. I asked him if he would like to attend the first night of *Eugene Onegin* at the Opera House. He looked me directly in the eye. It wasn't really his cup of tea. I appreciated him being Dad. Then his neighbour popped in, clearly expecting her afternoon cup of tea. I had known her for years and we chatted for a while until it was time I left.

I caught the 68 back to Holborn. I sat on the bus. It was quite empty before the afternoon rush hour. This was the same route I used to take when I did my degree and later as an academic. It allowed me to reflect on the changes since that time. Reflecting now on those thoughts, would I have rather followed a different path? I ask myself this now, writing as I am effectively a life story of a kind, because it is a question I have often been asked by other people. I think they view my working life with the Institute as a peculiar devotion. It was sterile; a fool's errand. The sterility was not something I realised at the time. Even now, I dislike the negative sense of being fruitless, although that description would be true.

Peter, I realised sitting on the bus, was the young man I had met with Herr Winter, the man who had lost his job because he had come out at his workplace. I did not know that Claude had kept in touch with him after he found him the job in the arts. Inviting him to the opening night was a foolish gesture on Claude's part. It would irritate Herr Winter. It would embarrass me. Nonetheless, it was Claude's decision and not my part to interfere. I felt narrow and lacking courage. Why did I not tell my dad about our relationship? Why did I not want to shock, or indeed believe that he would be shocked? My excitement and anticipation for opening night was a little dented. I did not care to ask had Claude also intended that.

Herr Winter and his wife and daughter were staying at the Goring. He invited me over and we had tea as he caught up on some business matters. His wife and daughter were shopping. The sixteen year old Friederike was consumed with excitement at the idea of attending the opening of a Winter sponsored opera in London. Her father was enchanted that his daughter was so completely enthralled. She was a perfect teenager. *Eugene Onegin* opened in two days' time. As a result, Claude was completely busy. I saw him only at night for the few hours he slept. There was a sense of great expectation that I shared with Herr Winter when he asked after the production. He was, I realised, giving himself a holiday. He wore a sports jacket and grey slacks, differing from his normally formal lounge suit. He looked like a merchant banker on holiday.

Herr Winter, his wife and daughter were the guests of the minor royals hosting the box for the great and the good attending this opening. I had my seat in the stalls and accompanied the costume designer with her guests, the brigadier and his wife. We were introduced to each other in the orchestra stalls bar over glasses of Champagne. Claude would watch the production from his own vantage point high in the gods from where he could make rapid trips back stage if required. He did not join us. He liked to be with the production staff at this time. I never saw him suffer any nerves. I never saw that with Claude. He was confident in the way that he was always sufficient to the occasion.

I recognised Peter by his awkwardness despite the crowd that made it difficult to move around. I excused myself from the other guests and with difficulty, made my way over to where he was standing. He didn't have a drink and I realised I still had my glass of Champagne. I gestured to him offering to get him a glass but he shook his head which was just as well as the chance of getting served at the bar was nil. We spoke easily enough. The job was working out well, although he still hoped to get a post with Claude's help at the English Speaking Theatre. As I sipped my Champagne, the bell went and the crowd began to make its way to the seats. We parted and I returned to find the others had already taken their seats so I followed on.

Before the lights went down, I glimpsed Herr Winter in the royal box. Their drinks and canapes were arranged on small tables at the side of the individual chairs – the same canapes we might be eating stale for lunch tomorrow in the canteen. I did not recognise the other members of the party. There was a sense of grand occasion and Friederike looked grown up in her specially designed dress. At the first interval, more Champagne awaited us. The brigadier was getting along well with the costume designer whom his wife complimented on the beautiful period costumes she had created. I smiled to remember the difficulty Claude had described of getting her to abandon the Dior suits and ball gowns. There was now no sign of Peter. I hadn't seen him in the stalls, so perhaps he was sitting in one of the circles. Claude had insisted I sat in the stalls, to be as close as possible to the action and to the music.

What we recall and what we imagine happening blur. I cannot really be certain if my memories of the opening night reception are any clearer or more accurate than my memory of the production. I know it was a deliberately traditional interpretation matching the superficiality of the form with the superficiality of the audience's expectation. There was the usual wild enthusiasm and overworked raptures at its conclusion. Beautiful bouquets and outrageous curtain calls vied with the audience's desire to believe in the importance of the occasion.

The reception, however, was not so straightforwardly extraordinary. For the reception was the occasion for the Winter Institute to reap the reward for its generous sponsorship and as such felt more like a business event. Claude, whom I had missed so much in recent days, was consumed by the Winter's requirement: not only as the director of their memorable *Eugene Onegin* but also as the newly appointed and acclaimed director of the English Speaking Theatre.

Like at a wedding, we queued to enter and be greeted by some of those I had glimpsed in the royal box earlier. The royals themselves had retreated to seats at the far end of the hotel ball room used for the occasion. Instead we shook the hands of Herr Winter, Claude and the Chair and Director of the Opera House. I had become detached from my companions in the theatre. I waited my turn. As I did so, Peter reappeared. He stood beside me. I felt I had no alternative but to accompany him as we made our approach to the welcoming committee. Claude beamed at me. He spoke warmly to Peter and turning introduced Peter to Herr Winter, reminding him of how they had come to meet.

Herr Winter nodded in his pleasantest way. He shook my hand and bowing his head to my ear congratulated me on Claude's success. It was all, I think he commented, he expected on behalf of the Winter Institute.

Friederike

Catherine opened the glossy red opera house programme for *Eugene Onegin* at the credits page. Claude's name was there as director. Turning through the pages, looking at the production shots and glancing at the articles about the opera, Catherine quickly understood the traditional tone adopted. Further through the programme was a full page notice from the opera house itself thanking the Winter Institute for its generous sponsorship and praising its philanthropic role supporting the arts. On the opposite page, there was an article describing the Institute's work written by Herr Winter whose photograph showed a man in his fifties with grey hair and an air of distinguished importance. There was a reference to the summer season at the English Speaking Theatre and the excitement as everyone looked forward to Claude's future productions.

    Alongside the programme and the invitations to the reception celebrating its opening night, Catherine found the newspaper reviews that had appeared. To her slight surprise the production had met with a luke-warm response. It was criticised for being too timid, for being afraid to lift the curtain on a deeper response to and understanding of the music. She wondered how Ben and Claude would have felt reading these neither damning nor glowing comments. The reviews did not refer to the Winter Institute. There was just a sense of disappointment. The production should have done much better, she felt reading them, especially given the creative talent of conductor and singers. It struck her as strange that Ben should preserve such negative testaments to Claude's operatic debut. Yet that is exactly the Ben she had learned to understand as she continued to make her way through the archived material. Everything to do with the Institute collated, labelled, indexed, retained.

She had arranged to skype Alain. It was a regular weekly event for the two of them now that she was spending so much time at the Bloomsbury flat. She had moved in, she explained to him, in a way that did not cause any disruption to the records. This left her with limited space for things and a sense of accommodating the past in this present, accommodating Ben.

Alain had not started at the Institute until after Claude's death in 1994, the year before the Hirschlich Centre had reopened in its adapted factory space at the western end of the Giudecca. Catherine had seen all the papers describing the opening. That was going to be the next big thing in her Ben story. As Alain had not known Claude, she was unable to glean from him a first-hand account of the man. He was clear in their conversations that Ben's grief for Claude had become a part of his personality. It seemed, he said, to preclude any other intimate connection.

Now, speaking with Alain, she held the 10x8 black and white production photos of *Eugene Onegin* in her hands. They were glossy and the sharp contrasts achieved by the lighting created a sense of the operatic theatre of the 80s. She held them up to the camera causing Alain to laugh. Could she send over copies, he asked. She assented.

What he did want to tell her about was Ben's infatuation with Friederike. Alain himself had never found Friederike a warm person. She had her business school degree and her fine arts background. Now she led the Institute, although her father remained a powerful influence as had Herr Winter senior in a previous era. Still, for Ben, Friederike had a charmed aura. Ben spoke with great pleasure of how she had appeared at 16, or not quite 16, at the premiere of *Eugene Onegin*. How she had praised the production and in her own way fallen in love with Claude. Alain's view, expressed to Catherine on that Skype chat, was that Ben's affection for Friederike was founded in that early appreciation of his late partner. She represented a possibility for Ben of what might have been achieved if Claude had survived.

Later Catherine would meet Friederike with Herr Winter when she eventually travelled to Versur. Friederike would be influential in the reception by the Institute of Ben's autobiography. Catherine hoped Friederike would see it as an artistic enterprise. She didn't reckon on Friederike, and Herr Winter, believing it was Ben's own work; his own story written by his own hand. Now Catherine needed to work on Venice. She returned the records of the *Eugene Onegin* production to the correct place in the archive. She extracted one box of papers about the newly restored Hirschlich Centre, including the Guide written for the occasion by Ben.

Welcome to the wonderfully restored Hirschlich Centre in the beautifully redesigned and reimagined industrial buildings here at the little visited west end of the Giudecca.

The Winter Institute is extremely grateful to the Venetian authorities for their support for the initiative. As a trading family, the Winters have a long connection with Venice based on their love for this historic city. That is why the Institute that now bears the family's name decided to show its collection of paintings entrusted to them by the former German dealer, Herr Hirschlich, in their Venice town house, also, incidentally, on the Giudecca reflecting the family's earlier industrial interests in the Veneto. It quickly became apparent that the family's home was not sufficient to allow the many visitors to the Hirschlich Collection to see it to best effect. It is a testament to the suffering of Herr Hirschlich as a victim of the Holocaust, that this new centre has been established in his name. We must never forget this as we honour and celebrate the breadth and extent of his wonderful collection.

Venice 1995

I love Venice. It was happenchance that the Winter Institute had an office in a place I so adored. It gave me many excuses to visit and I regularly boarded the train in Lyon on my way there. The journey was itself a pleasure, although long. It also gave me the opportunity to stop off at places along the way. I would spend nights in Italian and French cities: Milan, Bologna, Marseille, Nice. The trips would take a week or more. It seemed permissible as part of my role, especially as the Hirschlich Centre was itself there. My enquiries into the provenance of the Hirschlich Collection made little progress. There was instead a vacuum where such records should exist. When we were on the point of opening the new Hirschlich Centre in 1995 I had only the single written record from Leipzig. Herr Winter was tolerant of this lack of progress. He tended to shrug his shoulders and tell me that the efficiency and organisation of the Germans was an overdone prejudice. He seemed increasingly reconciled that my primary task, over and above collating the documentary history of the Winters and of the Institute, was going nowhere. "You are leaving no stone unturned, to use your very English expression," he said.

The opening of the new Centre was planned for May 1995. The planning had been meticulous. Outstanding project management of the scheme meant that the Centre was in fact ready to open when I was there on my final preliminary trip in January that year. If you have never been in Venice in January, then you have missed a wonderful opportunity to see the city without crowds and in the wonderful ambience and silence of a Venetian winter. Despite the floods, when you learn why Venetian calendars all give the times of high and low tides, it is possible to appreciate the rhythm of a great city on its own terms and to imagine its past without the pageantry of tourism gone mad. That was the case that January but all overshadowed by the death the year before of Claude. Less than 12 months had passed and I already knew that I would bear the grief for his loss for the rest of my life. It is easy to write this down as if it is just some fact about myself, which it is. It is much more difficult to convey, I believe, the reality of a feeling of enduring loss that is itself of the same substance if the opposite of the enduring love that follows in the path of initial passionate rapture. Grief and rapture weighing equally in the balance as a sign that defined my own personal circumstance in love.

When in Venice I stayed in a small pension in Ste Croce, not far from I Frari and also convenient for the station and Piazzale Roma. I eschewed the grand hotels used by the other staff of the Institute. The family naturally used their own house on Giudecca now that it had been released from its duties formerly housing the Hirschlich Collection. Friederike, the beautiful, talented and lovely Friederike who had first delighted me with her appearance at Claude's opera production, had arranged to meet me at my hotel. I sat not sure what to expect in the dining area now emptied of the few other guests staying at this time of year. In fact the hotel had only reopened this week after closing for a month over Christmas.

Friederike arrived and was charmed by the hotel. As she normally had access to the Winter family launch, I was intrigued why she had come here to meet me. We drank cappuccino and she explained, charmingly, that she wished to experience Venice as a tourist and she believed I would be the perfect guide. I felt honoured and admitted that I thought myself an excellent choice. I was determined to rise to this challenge. Would she be happy to take the rather lengthy walk over to the Nuove Fondamente and then the ferry to Torcello? We might have to change at Burano as we were out of season, despite Friederike's desire to spend a day in persona turistica. She was delighted by the idea, having walked here already from the crossing point where the Winter launch had dropped her next to the Gesuati. She warned me as we put on overcoats and scarves that it had been really foggy. We set off in the cold which meant we did not speak much as we made the 30 minute walk over to the ferry stop.

The ferry I had been aiming for was not running. I realise it was only available during the summer and consequently also that I had never been across the lagoon to the islands during January. Friederike was delighted that we were both experiencing our tourist trip together for the first time. Instead of the summer time ferry we were crammed with Venetians on to a vaporetto and as I had thought, would need to change at Burano for the short hop to Torcello. Sat side by side in the crowded vaporetto, everyone steamed slightly. The condensation on the windows obscured the view but as we speeded up across the open lagoon it became obvious that the mist was still so thick that there was virtually no visibility in any case. The boat, travelling quite quickly, must have been feeling its way through this dense mist. Friederike looked excited. It was exciting.

It was already nearly midday by the time we reached Burano. The mist had lifted, but not enough to be able to see Torcello. We had a 30 minute wait for the boat across. We stood by the seafood fritter counter and drank coffee out of paper cups. The conversation was trivial. Mainly, as I recall, Friederike's sense of adventure. This was her day of being a tourist. When we reached the cathedral on Torcello walking along the canal from the vaporetto stop, she was not disappointed. She took some photos of the cathedral in the now slightly lessening mist and then we went inside. We had the building to ourselves. Cold and damp the mist felt like it was drifting through the arched magnificence of the mosaics that shone despite there being so little light. We lingered, no longer chatting but separately involving ourselves in the historic magnificence. At least I was. I did not know how Friederike experienced the building. When we left she exclaimed her sense of awe. She explained that one experience like that was enough for her for one day of tourism. Venice was, she felt, too overwhelming although it was her intention to spend the winters here from now on in the Winter residence. She would explore the soul of Venice slowly. The summers would remain for her Versur.

It was the winter I wanted to avoid. In the winter, Claude went off on his skiing trips. He sought recklessness on the slopes in the winter. It was a different way of experiencing his sense of isolation. That first winter after his death, skiing to his death deliberately or half deliberately, I was in Venice with Friederike who adored and admired Claude so much. She took my hand. It was part of her joyfulness at the idiocy of our day out. There were, I wanted her to know, other tourist pleasures than art. It was time for lunch.

All the places on Torcello that would have swarmed with tourists in the summer had shut up shop. It was hardly surprising as only one other couple had joined us as we made our way round the cathedral. Four tourists today. We headed back to Burano. Walking past the seafood counter we went along the canal to the main street with its cute painted houses. Friederike wanted seafood. As we neared the main canal, we realised the water was flooding onto the pavement. Edging round this, we reached a bridge that took us to the other side of the canal which was not flooded. We did not know or, I think, care much whether the whole pavement would flood. We were ill prepared unlike the Venetians who had wading wellingtons in preparation for the inundation.

She chose the prettiest restaurant with pink and white tablecloths matching the plastic flowers in the local glass vases. We were too late really for lunch, but the restaurant served us anyway. It was nearly empty and we were a focal point for the waiters' attention. They estimated correctly that we were in holiday mood and there was good money to be made. The food was excellent. Our starter was a shared dish of all those little deep fried fruits de mer that I always associate as the most Venetian food. Afterwards Friederike had the langoustines and I the seafood risotto. We drank a half bottle of the most expensive white wine on the list.

In advance of our day out, sitting waiting in my little pension, I had been intimidated by the thought of what Friederike wanted from me. Although I had always seen her as my little girl, there was no acknowledgement of this on her part. It was just my fantasy based on the pleasure I had received seeing her at the opera ten years before. Our paths crossed only because of her admiration for Claude. This was tolerated by her father but not encouraged. Despite this, she worked each summer in the English Speaking Theatre and Claude found her useful. She was highly educated, organised and he appointed her, when she had finished at business school, in his usual ostentatious manner, as his Deputy Director. What she knew about directing remained unclear but there was no doubting her ability to get things done which was an invaluable skill in the hullabaloo of production week.

Despite my anxiety over a day with Friederike, I was now enjoying myself. I genuinely believed that I had given Friederike a unique experience that in her own world would be impossible. Through my eyes she had experienced Venice as a regular tourist might. She was eager to thank me, especially for the suggestion of Torcello and the wonders of being on the lagoon in the mist. It was, naturally, my pleasure and I meant this in a real way as I was enchanted to see Friederike was not too distant from the schoolgirl I had lost my heart to back in London.

I was not prepared for her next request. Later it makes sense. She knew me as Claude's partner. Although her father required us to be discreet it was obvious to everyone in Versur that we were a couple living together. We saw each other at parties. Otherwise her work for Claude did not mean our paths met. My fantastical elevation of her was simply an indulgence that I need take no further than as part of my romance with the Winter family itself. Perhaps that was why I was concerned spending time with her might break the spell.

As we reached the end of the main course her mood changed. She became serious and requested I listen carefully to what she wanted to say to me. I was taken aback. Her seriousness added to the attractiveness of her charm. She wanted, bluntly, to know if I would approve if she became the next director of the English Speaking Theatre. She was clear. She felt it was important to respect Claude's memory and the only way she could do this was to seek my permission.

I was touched. I concealed, I believe, my doubt that she was the right person to follow in his footsteps. There was no trace of my scepticism that she could possibly have the right level of creative genius such a role required. I felt, even as I listened to her, that I could rely on the Institute and on her father to make sure this never actually happened. So, enchanted by Friederike, by our day together, by the outrageousness of her idea, I told her I could not think of anyone more suited or suitable to take on from where Claude had so tragically been cut off.

I could see she was delighted. She again reached across the table to put her hand on mine and tell me I was a darling or some such endearment. It was impossible not to be charmed by her and I indulged my delight. I also now could imagine Herr Winter similarly reacting with indulgence to his daughter's wish. He would find some way of compensating for her inexperience and probable lack of talent – guest directors, someone behind the scenes pulling the strings. It was Herr Winter's special talent to enable those he valued. I think I must have smiled because the first of the two bombshells arrived.

"I am so glad," she said, "Peter said and looked exactly the same."

My mind stumbled hearing these exact words. Peter. I was less able to conceal my puzzlement and she picked up on it.

"Peter, you know, Peter who was on the skiing trip, who was at Claude's memorial in Versur."

So now I knew.

Friederike insisted on paying and I didn't mind. This was a one off, not the start of some wonderful friendship with the boss's daughter. I ensured my mood remained upbeat, but this was now manufactured whereas before it had been from my heart. She asked one of the waiters to take our picture together outside the restaurant. She gave me a copy when she had had the film developed.

Claude's memorial service at Versur had been a grand affair. It had all the hallmarks of the Winter Institute. The funeral had been a private family event in his home town in Switzerland. Herr Winter had been unusually frank in his discussions with me. The frankness was unusual but prompted by the tragedy of Claude's death. I should not attend. Claude's family loved him but strongly disapproved of his gayness. I would not be welcome. I must also stay away because if I did attend it would compromise the Winter Institute. This was the larger reason for Herr Winter's intervention. I reassured him I understood. My reward, a reading at Claude's memorial.

Claude would have been furious with me. I knew that. He would have been furious with his family whom he did love but rarely saw. They never came to see his productions at the English Speaking Theatre. How harsh those days were and now, in retrospect, how pathetic I was.

The memorial lasted an hour and took place in the theatre bedecked with floral tributes. Mainly it consisted of readings and eulogies from the great and the good. Mine simply melded in with the rest. There was also a short extract from his legendary production of Cardinal Richelieu with the original cast. It was staged by Friederike. That should have prepared me for her Burano declaration.

The second bombshell was Willi. He arranged to meet me in Harry's Bar. That was typical of the Willi I had known in Leipzig. The unforgettable Willi would not be forgotten. The message left at my hotel on the day I took the trip with Friederike to Torcello and Burano simply said, "I am usually at Harry's Bar late afternoon. Look me up. Yours affectionately, Willi (Leipzig 1985)."

He was sat at the bar as if he owned the place and I partly wondered if he did. The seat beside him was unoccupied. He stood when he saw me come in and gave me a bear hug greeting accompanied by his instantly recognisable laugh.

"You are here for the Hirschlich opening," he greeted me.

He did not tell me why he was there. He was in a great good humour and bought me a Campari and soda. I began to wish I had not come. He was no different. I doubted him. He did not tell me why he was in Venice. He had a familiarity with the Winter family and Institute that I found offensive. I had not expected to have such strong reactions to seeing Willi again. Now it was ten years later, ten years since the abortive trip to Leipzig. Willi knew I had returned in 1991. I don't know how he knew. He was always in the business of knowing. He was in Venice to see me. That information made me shudder. I felt hunted, under observation, under suspicion. Willi, still the police officer type, always having something on each of us. He was a spy before and still a spy now. Yet he wanted to be my buddy. The expensive drink in the clichéd bar was his opener.

What I also did not expect was the new information about Hirschlich. It would mean, Willi explained, a trip to Trieste. He suggested we went in the next couple of days. He had already spent some time there tracking down the Hirschlich connection. Although he did not tell me, I understood that he was on some kind of retainer from the Winter Institute. He was bringing his skills to bear where I had failed to make inroads in the Winter archives. His skills were of a more elaborate variety. He reminded me of the records we had found in Leipzig. He was unsurprised that they had vanished since reunification. So much had vanished, he told me as we sipped our drinks at the bar. His whole past had vanished, and he provided his trademark laugh as he said it. Willi vanished laughing.

We arrived in Trieste two days later in Willi's Mercedes. He told me on the trip that the best thing about reunification was being able to purchase and drive his own Mercedes. He had a firm commitment to everything German, meaning everything West German. It was just like his commitment to communism, he told me, but more enduring. He had chatted affably on the journey over as he drove. He was now, he explained, a consultant working for companies like the Winter Institute providing them with security advice and support. Security appeared to mean sorting out anything that wasn't playing favourably for the Institute. He was completely informed about the Winter's priorities. In fact, he admitted, showing a pinch of unexpected humility, that he was commissioned to find out as much as he could about Hirschlich that would be beyond my remit as the Winter Archivist. This, he felt, fitted well with our earlier encounter and he was, I think genuinely, pleased that we were back, as he put it, working together.

It was afternoon when we arrived in the city. I had not really known what to expect. The hotel was straightforward and old fashioned. It was more of a pension, more my kind of place, than the louche extravagance I associate with Willi. The hotel receptionist clearly knew Willi from previous visits and flirted slightly with him. I had forgotten that he was such an attractive man to women. I was finding it increasingly difficult to reconcile this Willi with the Willi I had met in Leipzig. The manner was exactly the same; self-deprecating, humorous, always taking charge. What was different was the absence of menace that had, I realised, so marked his presence in Leipzig and in the GDR. The menace was absent. It had been replaced by confidence in his manner; the confidence that he was now in charge.

Staying in the centre of Trieste, Willi arranged for us to meet at a local restaurant later for some food. He remained openly keen to spend time with me and continue to be my best buddy. I had not trusted him in Leipzig because he was working for what at the time had been an alien government. Now I did not trust him because of the man I was meeting. Willi was by his nature untrustworthy and I asked him directly over our bowls of pasta why I should in fact rely on what he had found here about Hirschlich.

If he was offended by the directness of the question, it did not show. He laughed, of course, when did he not. His simple reply was why would I not trust him. He had shared the intelligence he had gathered only two weeks ago with Herr Winter. Herr Winter had indicated that he should bring me here to corroborate this. Herr Winter had been the one to explain I would be Venice in preparation for the Hirschlich Centre opening. It was a good opportunity.

The guide to the Hirschlich Centre that I had been revising in preparation for the opening was in its final version. I did not know whether Herr Winter intended me to use the new information in the guide. To date I had only referenced Hirschlich as the art dealer whose collection had been entrusted to the Winter family in the years before the war when Hirschlich had to all intents and purposes disappeared from the records. The assumption was always that he had been murdered by the Nazis. The collection was in its own way a reminder and testament to his loss and suffering and the Winter family's commitment to honouring his memory.

Willi did not shy away from any of this. What he had found was someone here in Trieste who had actually met Hirschlich during the war. That was the person we would be meeting the following morning. Willi could not help but look a little triumphant as he pulled out this rabbit of information as we were eating. Finally, he bragged, we will have the proof you have spent so much time looking for. Willi ordered cognac and coffee. I allowed him his triumph. Truly I was intrigued. Willi was just too much of a coincidence in this story.

We breakfasted late the next day. Willi had continued drinking in the hotel bar the previous night when I had gone to bed and was a little the worse for wear. It puzzled me how he could maintain his security advisor hat while still drinking so much. Like the Mercedes, reunification had afforded him a better quality of liquor. He did not appear to want for cash. I realised he had so far paid for the entire trip, meaning, as always, the Institute was paying for everything including his expensive tastes. Willi would have wanted to know why. I would just record the receipts somewhere for another person to puzzle over. Did Willi submit expense claims to the Winters. I knew in asking the question it would all simply be reflected in his lavish retainer. What a person to have become acquainted with.

We drove into the Italian countryside. The weather remained cold and there was a gentle drizzle. Twenty minutes out of the city we turned into a car park next to a country house that had been considerably extended and resembled a hotel. It was in fact a care home and it was one of the residents here that we were coming to meet. Just as in the Trieste hotel, Willi was welcomed by the reception staff who clearly knew him from his previous visits. We were asked to wait in one of the lounges as Signor Roberto was still being got up by the staff. We were offered coffee and accepted. The home was decorated like a hotel. It appeared expensive and it felt like we were being waited on, which we were.

We did not have to wait long after our coffee arrived, beautifully presented with tiny lemon and cream cakes. Signor Roberto was wheeled into the room where we were sitting by one of the assistants and then we were left alone. Willi went over to Roberto and shook him by the hand. Speaking quite loudly, he had previously mentioned that Roberto was quite hard of hearing, Willi introduced me. He reminded Roberto of their previous meetings and why I was interested to know more about Hirschlich.

Roberto spoke quietly. "The art dealer," Willi translated, "during the war."

I could not understand what Roberto was saying and he spoke quickly. He appeared alert and interested to tell us about Hirschlich. He was just a young man when Herr Hirschlich had turned up in Trieste. His mother ran a little pension and Hirschlich had checked in. It was after the war started, Roberto said. His mother knew Hirschlich was Jewish. That was one reason Roberto had such a clear memory of the man. Hirschlich had stayed about a month, but then judged he was in too much danger and needed to move on. His mother and Roberto agreed that they could never speak of Hirschlich or that he had stayed with the family. It was too dangerous. Roberto had himself been obliged to join the Italian army. He was pointed on that topic.

Roberto was sad when he spoke about Hirschlich. When the war was over, he regretted his mother and his own silence about Hirschlich. When his mother had herself died in the 60s, he had written a small piece for the local paper describing Hirschlich's visit. That article had appeared in the local paper and it was Willi's enquiries that had unearthed this and led him to Roberto. Willi had the newspaper article photocopied and gave it to me. It was in Italian and Willi quickly highlighted the key points of the story.

I wanted to know what kind of man Hirschlich had been. Roberto said he had only known him for a month. He was mainly interested in hearing about his life in Berlin and about the artists he knew and who exhibited in his gallery. Not that Roberto knew very much about art. He was fascinated by the idea of Berlin, of living in a large city and of being a young man there. Now in his eighties, Roberto shrugged a little when he spoke of his own feelings and ideas at that time of his youth. It hadn't mattered. Herr Hirschlich was one amongst many, just one whose path had crossed with his own.

I remember asking if it was OK to go out into the gardens of the home. It was cold and we went back to Roberto's room where we helped him on with a coat, scarf and gloves. We wheeled him ourselves down the ramp at the back of the home into the attractive, mature garden. As it was January it felt a little bleak. This is where I photographed Roberto, in his wheelchair, with Willi standing beside him. When the photo was developed, Roberto looked more hunched and sadder than I remember. Willi has a huge smile – the visual equivalent of a thumbs up. For him it was a good moment. For myself, I felt at the time, it was outside what I had been commissioned to do by the Winters. I was not, like Willi, a police sleuth tracking down unlikely clues in out of the way places. I was just the recorder of known and documented facts. I carefully folded the photocopied newspaper article in my inside pocket so that I could catalogue it later as part of the collection.

After thanking Roberto we drove back to Trieste. Willi was keen for lunch. It was a cold day and mainly I wanted something warm to drink. We went into a café and Willi ordered spaghetti. I had a coffee. He was keen we carry on with our investigation, his word. Roberto said Hirschlich had told him that he was going to Zagreb. Hirschlich thought Zagreb might be safer, more out of the way, somewhere he could hide out during the war. Roberto was surprised Hirschlich believed that the war, the Nazis, would end. No one thought that in Trieste.

Willi was all for driving straight on to Zagreb, checking more newspapers, seeing if we could find a trail. I did not want to accompany him. The chance of finding anything was impossibly remote. Not only was it more than half a century ago but Hirschlich himself had the strongest reasons to be as invisible as possible. I had asked Roberto to describe Hirschlich to us physically. It was too long ago. He couldn't remember anything particular about his appearance. The standard grey suit and hat of any man of that period, always in black and white as he remembered it more in the stereotypes of the time than actualities of individuals. There was no photo. This now I found more frustrating than anything. How could someone alive in the 30s, someone who ran a successful gallery in Berlin, have disappeared so completely.

Willi found me too pessimistic. He criticised me for giving up, as he saw it. If I would not accompany him, then I must make my own way back to Venice. He was definitely going to follow up Roberto's report and look for the long gone Hirschlich in Zagreb.

Nonetheless we parted on friendly terms. It was impossible for Willi not to be good humoured and therefore equally impossible for me not to wish him well and thank him for tracking down Roberto. He left that afternoon in his Mercedes and I was left to sort myself out.

I checked in for an additional night at the hotel. My idea, rather romantically, was to return to Venice by ferry. The hotel receptionist, with limited English, was no help in identifying a ferry company, so I took a taxi to the ferry terminal. Here, hard against the grey of the Adriatic, everything was silent. I had expected the bustle of a port, but the steel doors were shut and there was a deep silence. I found the terminal office, but it was closed. I looked at the published timetable. The ferries started in April and only ran until October. There did not even appear to be a direct route between Trieste and Venice. The taxi had gone after dropping me off, so I had to walk some way towards the city before finding another taxi to take me back to my hotel. My romantic ferry trip had to be postponed indefinitely. The train, which was direct, took less than three hours.

I did not see Friederike on my return to Venice. Our paths did not cross. We did not actively avoid each other. There was simply no opportunity to renew the slight intimacy of the trip to Torcello. The guide was at the printers, the proofs approved by Herr Winter himself who had sent me a congratulatory telegram. Trieste was even by then an odd memory. I did not speak of it to Herr Winter. I collated the photocopied newspaper article about Hirschlich's alleged stay with Roberto's family in Trieste. There is no reference to it in the Hirschlich Centre Official Guide. I restrained the references to Hirschlich to the limited facts of the endowment to the Winter family as entrusted in the event of Hirschlich's decease. That was it. I returned to Versur.

The Centre opened, as planned, after Carnival and before the height of the summer season. Then as now, the Centre is one of the great cultural experiences of the city. For some a welcome relief from Venice itself.

Peter

Catherine placed the two photos she had been working from most recently on the desk in front of her. She had paused in her writing. She felt badly about some things. The writing had fallen into a habit. She relied too much on the photos, not enough on diligence. On the back of the photo of Friederike outside the restaurant she had identified in Burano she read Ben's note: "Where Friederike told me about Peter." A clue is different from evidence. She criticised her laziness. She needed to dig deeper. There was in her approach an absence of thoroughness. It was an insult to the comprehensiveness of Ben's approach. Yet, she was prepared to remonstrate with herself, he had been the archivist. She was the one who had taken on the task of bringing Ben to life. To bring Ben to life she also needed to bring so much more to life. That is why the photos helped her most. She needed all the time to imagine Versur, the Hirschlich Centre, Friederike and her intimidating father Herr Winter. People and places combined with the events that had shaped this life of record keeping.

The other photo was of Willi. She recognised him from before, from the snap in Berlin when Ben had visited there with him. He was obviously older because he was now quite bald. Beside him, in a wheelchair, was the man they had met in Trieste. Nothing written on the back of this photo. It was filed with Ben's detailed hand written notes of the meeting and the newspaper cutting that had led Willi to his witness. Then the archive had simply stopped. Stopped at Zagreb. In fact stopped short of Zagreb. She had questioned Alain the last time they had skyped about Willi and Zagreb. Alain disliked speaking about Willi. He acknowledged that he had known him but really he had known more about him than knowing the person. His influence at Versur was, Alain believed, considerable. Yet, Willi belonged to a realm of influence that was much closer to the family than it was to the Winter Institute.

It was exactly these comments which excited Catherine's interest the most. The archive could only take you so far. There was the necessity of imagining the past and the life Ben led for so many years in his job back then. Alain was the closest thing she had to an interpreter and guide. Now, she knew, it was nearly a year since she had embarked on this task. Her conversations with Alain had become more frequent and she felt, intimate. This was not an intimacy of romance. Instead it was the intimacy of a shared quest. Alain, sceptical to begin with, now insisted on hearing how she was progressing. She knew it was slow by his standards. Yet she needed time to consider, to review, to rework her conclusions or working hypotheses. Most of all she needed time to read in the archive. She collated the various strands of meaning into her story.

She was disappointed that Ben in her story failed, in her mind, to cut the figure she had hoped for. In her version of Ben he lacked distinction and appeared drab. That word concerned her. Drabness was not something she wished to endow her creation with. He would never be, and she would never wish him to be, cavalier or showy. Yet, he lacked a dynamism that having known him in real life she felt she was doing him an injustice. Alain again helped. His recall was of an affectionate man; a man whom he trusted – both his judgement and his integrity. Still, as Catherine looked at the photos and reflected, that remained insufficient to create the person she had known.

Of course, what Alain most wanted was to read her manuscript. That would have to wait. Nearly a year on from the start of the enterprise, she was not ready for another reader. Alain tried to help her narrow her focus on Ben. He told her at length of the last few days in Lyon before Ben had returned to London and the flat in Bloomsbury. He knew how it had ended with the Winters. Ben had been specific and shown him the letter terminating his employment. Catherine had already read it in the archive. He knew that it had been a painful ending, although that might be inevitable after such a long time. It was clear to Alain, when he had travelled each day for nearly a week to meet with Ben in Lyon, that Ben was devastated. He was completely unready for the termination of his duties. His fidelity to the Institute had been utterly repudiated. It was, in Alain's opinion, the intention of Herr Winter to break any bond irrevocably. There could be no doubt in Ben's mind that his service was concluded and he had no right of return. What remained unclear was why this had happened. Why at this time and why in this manner.

Alain was clear that a major reason for Ben wanting to talk this over with him was to warn Alain about the Winters. He had been inexact, but the essence was that Alain should not fall into the trap Ben had of a complete reliance. Alain told Catherine that this was hardly news. The Winters were ruthless in their own way. Ben was well rewarded and there was no question over being provided for in every way even after the break from the Institute. That was how the Winters always worked. What damaged Ben was the abrupt finality of his exclusion. Alain, as he told her, had never bought in so completely to the Institute. He had chosen to live in Grenoble and commute to Versur. For him, it was a job – a job he enjoyed – but not a calling. It was, he thought, a reason he remained in regular contact with the Winters despite having stopped working there a few years after Ben. Friederike was in regular contact. She now spent a reasonable amount of time herself in the Winter's Grenoble home.

Alain was thinking of visiting Catherine in London now that the anniversary of Ben's death was approaching. He wondered aloud to her whether he could see a draft of what she had been writing before he came over. She said it might be possible for him to receive a copy when he visited, or instead she could come to see him. She asked him about Peter.

Alain didn't know about Peter. Other than the photo and the formal references to Peter in relation to his employment, there was no more information. Catherine wondered if he too had disappeared. He had a walk on part in the story. He confirmed Ben's understanding of a betrayal that had insisted on a life in Versur that in the end added up to a lie.

Lyon 2011

I have retired. Thirty-one years after my appointment as the Winter Archivist at the Winter Institute, I have retired. I am 55 years old. Now my work has finished. I cannot pretend it is other than an abrupt ending. The Institute has ensured that I shall not be impoverished in my retirement. Quite the reverse is the truth. I already own the Bloomsbury flat. Now I shall have an excellent income and a considerable payment in cash in addition. Herr Winter wanted me to understand exactly how grateful they are for all my services. I should be, and I am, grateful.

There was no send off. I am a reasonably quiet man so I was grateful. I was surprised so little was made of my departure. It is after so many years of service. Friederike, who has always been so kind to me, presented me with a small gift in her office. It was one of the original copies of the guide I wrote to Versur when I first arrived. It was a lovely thought. I do naturally already own a number of copies of the original guide, each in better condition than the one pressed on me by Friederike. It is the thought that counts. I also have my own archive of papers in the Bloomsbury flat. That is a slight thing. It is merely a personal, and a little sentimental, collection of the papers I have assembled as I have toiled in the Winter archives. It is a story well worth telling and one that I hope one day to have the time and talent to attempt.

For 31 years I felt I enjoyed a close and unique relationship with Herr Winter and, through him, with his family and the Institute that encapsulates their dedication to culture and peace. Just one month ago, Herr Winter invited me to what he described as a more formal meeting with him in his office. I was intrigued to know what this might mean. Generally, we chat when we see each other. If I need his opinion or direction, I can readily gain access to him through his secretary. I am a regular and trusted confidant.

In his office in Versur we did not on this occasion sit on the sofas where we were in the habit of conferring. Instead, we were seated at the more formal table. Also present was a lawyer whom Herr Winter introduced. I have known a number of the lawyers used by the Institute, but that is an area of its work I rarely have need of. The lawyer and I greeted each other politely. Clearly we were seated at the table as the lawyer needed somewhere to spread out his papers. I waited for Herr Winter to begin proceedings, still intrigued as to what might be about to happen. To my surprise, Herr Winter invited the lawyer to speak.

The lawyer explained that he had a letter for me from the Institute. This letter was addressed to me. It contained details of the termination of my employment with the Institute and detailed benefits I would receive in addition to the generous (that was his word) pension I would be receiving immediately my employment was concluded. Time was of the essence. It was imperative to the Institute that this matter be resolved immediately. They could brook no delay. The suggestion, or rather instruction, I received, was to read the letter while the lawyer and Herr Winter withdrew for 20 minutes, so that I would be in a position to sign a copy as the contractual termination of the employment. One of the secretaries was ready to act as the witness to my signature.

Herr Winter smiled warmly as the lawyer concluded his explanation. The letter was passed across the table to me in a pink folder. Herr Winter stood and smiling benignly, lent over the table to shake my hand before he and the lawyer left the room.

Let me be straightforward. This came as a complete shock. It was wholly unwelcome. I think I would be truthful if I said it was the worst thing that ever happened to me. It was not only the fact, but the manner in which it happened. I cannot to this day fathom why I was treated in such a manner. I signed the letter. Later, when I discussed the issue on numerous occasions with Alain, he chided me for giving in so easily, I always felt there was no choice. I was not told an alternative. Yet I knew unadvised that any alternative would be a worse option for me. I always knew this side to the Institute existed. Indeed I would find myself defending the family's at time ruthless behaviour. It was necessary to maintain the clarity of the Institute's work. Threats should be dealt with effectively and without regret. Yet I had never expected to be such a threat. Nor am I now.

I did read the papers before I signed them. It was a simple letter taking up three sides. It detailed the substantial and generous financial arrangements, including a significant compensatory severance payment in addition to an enhanced pension for the rest of my life. I would certainly be comfortable financially. It also laid out the conditions on which the offer was made. I was and am subject to a confidentiality agreement which prohibits me absolutely from speaking, writing or in any way commenting on any aspect of the work of the Winter Institute. Furthermore I was obliged to return any papers relating to the Institute, originals or copies, that were in my personal possession. The penalty for any failure to comply with these conditions was the right of the Institute to void the agreement. Essentially to cut me off without a penny. So the whole of this document is in breach of my contract of dismissal. My personal archive of Winter Institute materials in Bloomsbury, carefully collated over so many years, another breach. It makes me feel like a criminal. I had carefully created a personal facsimile of the Institute archive in Bloomsbury as a possible hobby for retirement. How crass that idea now seemed. My hobby, my extra work for the Winters I had intended to undertake on their behalf out of my continued interest and loyalty was itself now criminalised.

Alain referred to the conditions as draconian. Fortunately he did not know about the Bloomsbury archive. It is a great relief to me that he does not know as it would place him in a difficult position. I do not want to force any split in his loyalty between me and the Institute. That is largely selfish. For if there is such a split, I must advise him to stick with the Winters. Not only in his own interest, but because I have spent so much time working to prepare him to take on my role.

The lawyer came back into the room as he had promised twenty minutes later. He was no longer accompanied by Herr Winter. I realised that I would not see Herr Winter again. The lawyer showed no sign of stress. This time he was accompanied by one of the junior secretaries from Herr Winter's office. He came and stood beside me and looked over my shoulder at the paper. I had not stood. My pen was poised to sign and he nodded. I dated my signature. The lawyer beckoned to the secretary who walked around the table and without sitting, bent over to sign where the lawyer indicated. There were two copies of the papers. The secretary left the room and the lawyer – I never knew his name as we had never been introduced – folded one copy of the now signed and witnessed letter into a brown envelope which he presented to me. I thought that was the end of the formalities. I was wrong.

Having handed me the envelope, as I was rising to depart, the lawyer put his hand on my shoulder indicating that I should remain seated. He walked back round the table and sat facing me. He spoke with the confidence I had only minutes before enjoyed in the same room.

I was to understand that my notice period of four weeks as set out in the letter should be spent in my office packing away any outstanding papers. Access to the archive itself was not allowed. Alain, my assistant, would be with me at all times when I was in my office. If I needed anything from the archive or from any other part of the building, Alain could fetch it for me. As I lived in the apartment at Versur, time might also usefully be spent packing up my things. The Institute would arrange transport of my possessions to the UK where, the lawyer explained, he understood I had a flat in London. I nodded. I could, of course, use the restaurant and other Versur facilities as usual. He smiled. He thanked me for my cooperation. His thanks were genuine. Maybe in these situations it was not always so easy. Herr Winter, he said, had assured him that I would be well disposed to see the advantages of the offer I was being made by the Institute. I nodded. It was, I commented, very generous. I did, however, have one question. The lawyer's slight smile of approval hardened momentarily. I hoped, I went on, it would be in order for me to conclude my affairs a little more quickly as I had been planning to take a short holiday in Lyon and would like to do this before returning to London.

I understood this to be completely in order. He went to the door and held it open for me to leave.

I remember sitting in the drab one star hotel I had found on the internet booking site. It was near the theatre. The door to the hotel was difficult to find in the street below as the sign had been worn and it was a narrow entrance between a shop selling hardware and a dry cleaners. Reception was on the second floor reached by the winding staircase of a traditional French townhouse. This one now converted on its upper storeys to become the hotel. I had never stayed in Lyon before. I had no need to as it was easily reached from Versur. The hotel was run by a family. I have come to know them over the years since as I often use this hotel for my trips to catch up with Alain in Grenoble.

I only stayed two weeks more at Versur before I came here. Alain was and is the great companion of my demise; my Winter demise. He continues to work for the Institute. What else should he do? First at Versur and now in my drab hotel in Lyon, he supports me. It is quite subtle. He does not pity me. I have been completely open with him about my dismissal. He says that word is not correct. He prefers to speak of my retirement. It is a forced retirement. I have shown him the letter, when we were still in Versur. He has read it carefully. I can see he is shocked by it. Soon, however, he is changing his response. He tells me of the positive benefits. He laughs as he congratulates me on my financial position. It is true, I agree, I shall be able to take the best seats at the opera when I am living in my flat in London. He knows enough about Claude to go silent. He knows what I am really thinking.

Sitting in the hotel – there is no fridge just a shower room – I eat out mostly as there is no restaurant in this sort of hotel – I am mindful of the last meaningful event in Versur. Alain was keeping his guard over me. That was the term he used, jokingly but truthfully. One of the assistants from the English Speaking Theatre came into my office. She told us that Frederika wanted me to pop by. Now, if that wasn't too inconvenient. I was surprised. Since the theatre counted as other facilities at Versur, it was not off limits to my newly restricted self so I made my own way over there promising Alain to return to the office when I had finished so he could keep his eye on me. He bowed as I left.

I have to say Friederike has proved herself an agile and successful director of the English Speaking Theatre. She has now done the job so long it is difficult to think back to Claude's stunning seasons. They are remembered, but as something magically unrepeatable. They have, and I am gratified by this, become part of the mythology of the place. The theatre itself, it is my opinion, is in a gentle but irrevocable decline. Friederike's boldest innovation is the summer season of gay theatre that has established itself as an annual subject of pilgrimage for the right crowd. I know it is her testament to Claude. She loves me, I think, because she loved him so dearly. Her own father, whom I shall not see again, understood Claude's importance to his daughter and has found the gay themed theatre as a useful cosmetic for the Institute as it adjusts to a role in the current century.

I realise that I am in any case being escorted to Friederike's office by the assistant who opens the door so that I can enter immediately and meet with her. She is sitting by her desk which faces a wall covered with posters for shows she has commissioned or directed. She swivels round in her chair and I can see she is sad. That is when she gives me the guide. This, I realise, I shall be able to keep. They are for the public.

Alain wanted me to come and stay with him in his gorgeous flat in Grenoble. He had never taken up the opportunity to live in Versur. At first I had frowned on his decision. It had led me to doubt whether I had made the right decision appointing him as my deputy, and I presumed; in due course my successor. As he was already living in Grenoble, I could understand he did not want the disruption. The competition for the post had not been quite as fierce as I had expected. Herr Winter had put out feelers in his usual way. The academics he had approached made vague suggestions of potential researchers they were supervising. However, the allure of the Institute appeared less appealing than it had to me. As ever the financial rewards and other benefits, like an apartment at Versur, were significant. They did not, however, attract anyone away from the harsher and more rigorous requirements of university careers in whichever country Herr Winter approached his professors. The job, I consoled myself, was not as senior as my own. The ground had already been cultivated by me. Perhaps no one wished to be in my shadow.

Alain in any case had excellent credentials. Working at a senior level in the Musée des Beaux Arts in Grenoble, itself now in the splendid modernist building Herr Winter had advised the President on, he was extremely knowledgeable and as far as I could judge, shared my enthusiasm for the cultural and educational role of the Institute. We became over the many years we worked together good friends. More than colleagues, Alain is the person I relied on most when my tenure at the Institute was so abruptly severed. Yet, I did not want to stay with him. Grenoble was too close to home. It was where I had first met the Winters, Herr Winter and Herr Winter senior. Where my Winter adventure had commenced. I knew Friederike regularly resided in the Winter's Grenoble town house which was a mere ten minutes' walk from Alain's flat. Instead I preferred to spend time at the pokey Lyon hotel I had found. I wished, I told Alain, to explore Lyon for a week while my belongings were shipped to Bloomsbury. Then I would live there and get a dog. I would learn Italian, properly.

Alain sought and obtained my permission to be my companion of this week of visiting. He travelled over each day on the train having taken holiday from the Institute. I think he was keeping an eye on me, not sure how well I was doing after the blow of my forced departure. What I wished to communicate to him was not to become, as I had, so over reliant on the Winters, so vested in the Institute that the gift a of a dog eared guide, however kindly meant, from Friederike, was more an insult than an affectionate token. Naturally I need not have worried about Alain any more than he needed to about me. So the time was pleasantly spent.

The plan for the day was to visit Vienne. We had previously been through the old city and the traboules and spent a separate day at the market in Saint Croix. By the time I reached the Part-Dieu station to meet Alain when he arrived from Grenoble, it was raining heavily. I think that is why I remember this particular day especially well. It was cold but

I had both a raincoat and an umbrella. I had not bought the tickets for the train to Vienne. Alain's train arrived late and we would need to get a move on if we were to catch the train in time for lunch there. At Alain's suggestion, we decided against the trip that day. It was too wet. We were late. We needed an indoor activity. Alain proposed the Musée des Beaux Arts. He knew a number of the staff there still from his days at Grenoble. It had a number of old masters he thought I would enjoy and the usual Picasso and the like. It was also, he pointed out, indoors.

Given the weather – the rain had intensified – I offered a taxi which we got into so we were at the museum in a few minutes. I did not bother to put up the umbrella as we dashed across the inner courtyard to the ticket office. None of Alain's friends was available, so we bought our tickets in the usual way and began our tour of the galleries. The museum was empty of people except for a school group of quite young children sat in front of a large religious painting by a slightly obscure Renaissance artist only vaguely known to me – I think he worked in Rome after the death of Raphael.

I had left my umbrella, still damp from my earlier walk to the station, and my coat in the cloakroom. We were both ready for a reasonably detailed session in the museum. Yet, I found the pictures unattractive. I was more impressed by the size of the galleries which did do justice to this selection of large oil paintings over the centuries. I was failing to concentrate and I shared my dilemma with Alain. He suggested a coffee and then trying the Greco-Roman section. When we reached the café on the first floor, it had not yet opened so we went straight on to the ancient exhibits. These were easier to assimilate than the rather stuffy old masters. I relaxed. I could see Alain was pleased I was more engaged with this part of the museum. Perhaps it better matched my expectations of visiting the temple in Vienne. I had read about the ruins there but even now I have never visited. I missed my chance that day.

After half an hour in the ancient artefacts galleries Alain came over and suggested we try another time for a coffee. I was grateful as I wanted to sit down. On the way to the café, which had now opened, Alain wished to show me one of his favourite pictures he remembered from working at the museum. He admitted he had not been here for some time, so wasn't even sure if the picture, the name of whose painter he could not remember, would still be there. We hovered around the nineteenth-century works and then Alain picked it out. Smaller than he remembered, it showed a man crouching under the cloth behind an old fashioned camera on a tripod taking a photograph of a newly married couple. It is clearly in the photographer's studio. There is a sense of celebration with members of the wedding group all dressed in fashionable nineteenth-century clothes sat watching the proceedings. The camera man has his back to us so that we gain almost the same view of the married couple as will appear in the photograph. The bridegroom is a little stout and he pouts a touch. The bride holds on to his arm. Neither appears especially attractive or well off.

It was a perfectly conceived work of art that immediately delighted me. It captured perfectly the effete bourgeois life of provincial France, the France that, like all European countries no longer exists but is close enough in time to imagine living there oneself. I don't know if it was intended as a joke, or at least a tongue in cheek conceit, but the idea of a painting of someone taking a photograph seemed to me witty and timely.

Before going to the café for our much delayed coffee, I wanted to see if there was a postcard of this painting and delightfully there was so I have for some time had it propped on the shelf in my flat in Bloomsbury.

The coffee was better than I had expected at the vaguely municipal room which was really part of the landing between the main parts of the museum. It was still raining I could see through the rather dirty windows by the staircase. I indulged myself in a croissant and Alain joined me. We munched. Alain drank his espresso in a single gulp and I sipped my coffee. We had already spoken of the move to the digitalisation of all the records at the Institute. It was well known that I was a hold out for maintaining a paper based record. Herr Winter, I believed, was persuadable but Friederike was on a drive to modernise. It was part of the plans she had to revamp Versur just as soon as Herr Winter allowed her. Alain had no strong views. What I could not disclose was that whatever happened, I had already created an alternative physical archive in Bloomsbury – an archive that now made me some type of criminal. I would not disclose my crime, nor would I destroy my personal archive. Quite the opposite. My treatment made me all the more determined to preserve it.

At the Musée des Beaux Arts, over our coffee and croissant, we did discuss Hirschlich. Alain's opinion was that my offence, if that was the right word, was to object so strongly to the invention of a back story for Hirschlich. Personally even now I do not believe that I was especially outspoken in the matter. I had a personal interest. Was it not true that my primary task was to establish the provenance for the collection now in the Hirschlich Centre? Was it also not true that the identity of Hirschlich was central to that provenance? Simply to overcome the difficulty encountered in finding any evidence for Hirschlich's existence by inventing him was for me diabolical.

I remember Alain laughing and almost choking on his croissant. I used that word, diabolical, as we talked the matter over. Did I not realise, he was suggesting, the word diabolical meant I took the matter very much to heart? Nonetheless my objections had been ignored and now, in the Hirschlich Centre Guide, the one originally authored by me, there appeared a pen portrait of the Jewish Art Dealer who had perished in the Holocaust leaving his precious collection in the care of the Winter Institute for the benefit of the world at large. Yet there was no shred of evidence to support this. Only the copied out pages from the Dresden records, the verbal testament of the man Willi had taken me to see in Trieste and the long ago article he had published in the local paper there when his mother died. Not enough, I think, not nearly enough.

The plan is working. I am now in my Bloomsbury flat. In fact I have the postcard of the painting from the Musée des Beaux Arts in Lyon propped on the desk here where I am writing. I have annotated, as I so often annotate these artefacts, with the date and time when I saw it and a brief note of the conversation with Alain. That day it was about Hirschlich, but more on that in a moment. For the record, the painting is called, *Une Noce Chez La Photographe* by an artist named Pascal-Adolphe Dagnan-Bouvert. He painted it in 1878. It is worth finding if you have a moment in Lyon to visit the museum. What an extraordinary name the painter has, with so many hyphens. I feel he is probably related to the people he has painted. They too look like members of the Dagnan-Bouvert clan.

I am learning Italian! I have a dog!

The Italian class is at the City Lit nearby, so an easy walk each Monday morning. I have joined a year two class. This felt risky. My Italian was less than rudimentary. Still, I am surviving. What I do not understand in the grammar is more than made up for by my speaking ability based on so many visits to Venice. I wonder when I shall go back there. Alain has been in touch regularly and is keen for us to visit there together or, if not too painful for me, to visit him in Grenoble. I think he is right. Grenoble is too painful. We have exhausted Lyon for now, although we never did make it to Vienne. Venice in the winter. That is best.

The dog is a stray I received from Battersea Dogs Home. This has been more of a trial. In the first place, my assessment as a suitable dog owner by the home was extremely rigorous. I did not resent this; the reverse in fact. It is clearly a good thing that stray dogs go to good homes. Second time lucky, so to speak. It was hard work. I attended a series of practical lessons on dog ownership and now have a certificate to demonstrate my competence. It was just as well as Willi – the dog's new name – proved initially a trial to settle in the flat. The flat was visited and there was a moment of hesitation on its suitability. I was able to win the argument by demonstrating that I am at home most of the time having retired and can afford to kennel Willi when I am away. I do not intend to travel very much. I am content to live here. I am reorganising the archive. I am myself taken aback by the amount of material I have squirrelled away over the years. It fills all two walls of shelves, one in my bedroom and one in the living room as well as a couple of filing cabinets and the desk drawers. The flat is not large, so the archive does present a bit of a logistical problem. Willi, however, enjoys hiding himself behind the various cabinets. I am glad he is properly house trained and we enjoy our walks in the local squares and parks. It is a little sad that he has to be on a lead most of the time. We do have excursions on the 24 bus to Hampstead Heath, avoiding the busy weekends, for a really good run. I think of Claude's story of the dog that ate the duckling in front of his costume designer. We met the dog's owner, a brigadier, and his wife at the opening night of Claude's stunning production of Eugene Onegin at the Royal Opera House.

Although the flat is small, cramped even, it has the advantage of everything being on hand. So I can immediately find the programme for that production together with the black and white press photos. With these I find the invitation to the Winter reception after the first night. I had forgotten that item, but of course it was the Winter Institute that sponsored the production. I enjoy leafing through the various papers before returning them to the folder. The new referencing system for the archive is proving very effective. I think for a moment what Alain would say if he visited here. He must not, of course, because he would shop me to the Winters and then there would be all hell to pay. Or would there? Perhaps I am just a forgotten ghost in Versur. I shudder as the name of the place slips through my mind. I leave it there. It is surely time for Willi's walk, or some revision of the latest grammar point in my Italian course book.

I have made a friend, a lady. Her name is Catherine and she is a potter who lives in Crouch End. On the pretence of an opportunity to practise speaking Italian, we are to have a coffee in the National Gallery café. I like her. We do practise Italian a little, but we both need to be rather better to learn much more from each other than where we live and what we do. I have explained I am retired, an academic is how I grandly describe my career at the Winter Institute. Not too distant from the truth, I believe. She is clearly interested that I live in Bloomsbury. I feel suitably caressed by her sensible approval for my fashionable address. The interest works both ways. I want to learn more about her pots. She tells me, we have moved into English by this stage, about the studio in the garden of her garden flat. How when it is too cold in the winter she has to work at the community college where she lectures. She tells me about her students. I wonder how good a potter she is and she replies intuitively that it is so difficult. Technically she is gifted. It makes her a good teacher. Creatively it is problematic to know. Her rule of thumb is to keep only the pots that she believes in. When I ask what she means by that, she laughs and says she cannot describe it in words, only pots. I think this is a good answer. I feel I am learning a lot about Catherine and that I like her very much. I hope she also likes me.

I have this idea but it is too soon to put it to Catherine. I need us to get to know each other more. I hit upon the idea of taking her to East Street back in Walworth. I want to show her, I explain, where I grew up. I have not been there for an age. My dad died himself a time ago. He survived my mum's sudden death but eventually, after a fall, was taken himself. I returned from Versur for the funeral and to sort out his limited affairs. He and Mum had always rented their home. There was so little left to sort out. His possessions were personal and worthless. He disappeared from view, like my mum, completely. I wondered about the bride and groom in the Lyon painting. Without the painting, they too would have disappeared completely. Photos disappear.

We walked through the streets where they had lived and I had grown up. Catherine drew the distinction between my job of archiving the Winter Institute and how untraceable my family has become now my parents have died. It was a sensitively made observation but not true. They exist on record unlike Herr Hirschlich. I was grateful for her tact and good sense. I become more confident each day that my plan is a good one. It is to ask Catherine to be the executor of my will. When I ask her in the following few weeks she eventually agrees. I do lie to her that I will make a small payment to her in my will as a thank you for her taking this on. She suggests there is every chance she will die first. It is possible. What I do not tell her is that I have decided to leave everything I own, including the flat, to her. There will be time enough for her to deal with this when I am gone.

This may appear whimsical. It is not. The only other person I can think of is Alain. Yet for me Alain, good friend that he is, remains too close to the Institute. He followed in my footsteps as the Winter archivist. My instinct makes me trust Catherine. I do not know how she will react or what she will do. I believe it will be interesting. If it is not, there is no harm. She will be the beneficiary of all this. Perhaps, like Hirschlich, it too will disappear without a trace. That is not quite true. It is not true at all. For Hirschlich is very solidly remembered and the Hirschlich Centre collection of twentieth-century art – the art he collected and passed to the

Winters – remains testament to that. It is the records for which there is no trace.

Willi has an excellent sense of smell combined with a furious desire to track down the source of any odour he detects, He should have been a police dog, like his namesake. He has no interest in games involving stick or ball throwing. I tried a few times when we have made it to Hampstead Heath to interest him in the art of retrieval of an object I showed him. Numerous other dogs were actively and happily engaged in this pursuit. But Willi showed no interest whatsoever. He ignored the thrown object not even bothering to look after it and usually walking slowly in the opposite direction, his nose to the ground. He was after a much more interesting and desirable object. He wanted to find what was promised by the scent on the ground before him. I explained from time to time that this meant he would always be disappointed. To my amazement this made no difference to him. Disappointment is not a dog feeling, not for this dog. I suppose he only remembered the chase, never the failure to find the quarry.

Our trips to the Heath were few. I came to the opinion that he preferred being on a leash. It meant that I could keep up with him. Practically, until I had worked out his preference for following his nose, I had nearly lost him up on the Heath. He moved fast. He did always eventually find me. I too had my own smell, and that smell meant food and shelter. On his leash, he could have the pleasure of straining against my will, or simply my ability to keep up with the quest. So today passers-by and tourists in Russell Square have been enjoying the sight of my dog tearing around the place with me hanging on as if I feared my dog was going to go straight under a bus. The weather was pleasant. Autumn, a warm and relatively dry autumn allowing a fine exhibition of the leaves in the drifting sunlight.

Willi keeps me fit and provides an excuse to get out into the open air. I believe that really Willi is leading me to some answer. As I walk and trot behind his willing, believing search, I think we will get there. I did not see the real Willi after Trieste. I know he was in touch with the Winters. There was no attempt to deceive me about that. It was mentioned openly. I learned, from Friederike, who else, that the scent had gone cold in Zagreb despite Willi's extensive investigations. I'm sure these were helped by his own background before the iron curtain came down. He would feel at home with anyone from Yugoslavia of old who had maintained the sense of total suspicion I had experienced so long ago now in Leipzig. If there had been any trace of Hirschlich, Willi would have found it. I imagined his irritation. Unlike Willi the dog, Willi would not forget the failure to track down Hirschlich, to run his quarry to ground. Willi would have the undoglike feeling of disappointment, or, I suspect, an anger that he, Willi, had somehow been thwarted by a smarter man or circumstance.

All of this is to presume that Willi himself believed the Hirschlich story and was not a part of its manufacture. I know I have had these suspicions now for so long. That is one reason I was so against the imagined character of Hirschlich that the Centre has now created to explain our famous German art dealer, but to explain really the cache of paintings gifted to the Winters. Willi finally exhausted himself this morning in the square and tired of providing entertainment for the people walking through, taking the diagonal short cut in either direction to the tube or to the museum. I was able to pause and sit down on one of the benches near the café which I do sometimes use for a filter coffee, reminiscent of my days in France. One of the staff in the café, not someone I recognised, brought a bowl of water out for Willi. We chatted briefly as I thanked him for the kindness. Dogs really do bring out the best in us. I promised to return the bowl when we went and did so buying a take away coffee in return for the kindness of the gesture.

Willi lapped at the water and then lay down, tired from his exertions. He appeared absurdly satisfied with himself. He had had a successful morning chasing nothing but his imagination. I hooked the leash under the foot of the bench although there was little likelihood now that tired Willi would want to do anything other than stroll gently home after enjoying his water and the warmth of the gentle autumn sunlight. I spent my time reflecting. I too needed to bring my search to an end.

The conclusion I have reached – it can be no more than a working hypothesis – is simple. Willi would have to have been in on it. I was hired simply to provide the illusion of the Institute searching for Hirschlich. The startling reality, or perhaps obvious to anyone who thought to enquire, is that Hirschlich is a fiction. It is convenient, more than convenient to the Winters and to the Institute that Hirschlich means there need be no problematic questions about how they obtained the Hirschlich pictures. It is true that the Winters were, as wealthy patrons, engaged in the art world in the 30s and would have known the major dealers. What appears now to me unlikely is that a collector with a back catalogue as extensive as Hirschlich's could disappear so completely.

Sitting on the bench, I began to share Willi the dog's composed satisfaction of a job well done. I wondered who had lived on the street in Leipzig. How Willi had invented the records that later so completely disappeared. How had the Winters known Willi when he was behind the iron curtain cut off from their world? How far did their influence run? Relaxed because now I could do nothing, I wonder if this is just an open secret – an open secret amongst the groups of people who are part of the Winters and their coterie. I try not to extend the hurt I felt at my last meeting with Herr Winter to a more general hurt, of loss of self-respect, of having been the dumb patsy for the whole affair. Friederike must know, or not. I savour that thought. I wanted to share Willi the dog's oblivion to the purposelessness of all that endeavour.

We walked back to the flat. I dropped the undrunk coffee into a bin as I did not now want it. The day was so beautiful, I wanted to forget Hirschlich, forget the Winters, even forget Friederike. As I now sit at my desk, back in the flat, pondering on what to do next with these ideas and conclusion, I want to remember instead Versur and Claude. Really I have known all this about Hirschlich for a long time. I certainly knew it when Willi came up with Senor Roberto. I could hear his distinct laugh as he told Herr Winter of how the idea had worked so perfectly in practice. The imagined art dealer refugee trying to disguise his Jewish identity. The more terrible truth of fabricating a lie on the back of monumental human suffering. I should not be surprised, but I had refused to admit the only reasonable conclusion instead wanting myself to continue to believe until my own belief became a problem and I was disposed of.

I remember Versur. It was the summertime. A group of us were enjoying the beautiful weather. I do not remember their names. We sat around a table out of doors. It was the end of the day but still very hot. Now though it was a pleasure to sit out of doors whereas earlier it had been too hot. There was always the possibility of a cooler breeze from the hills on a summer day in Versur. We sipped glasses of rosé, which is what we always drank on those summer days. I was so much younger and I felt being young with those other people – students, interns, people of my own age. The door of the English Speaking Theatre across from where we were sitting opened. I don't know why, but we all paused in our conversation, maybe six or seven of us grouped around the same table, and all looked across at where the door had opened. Coming out into the sunshine, I saw Claude for the first time. I could not then believe how beautiful he was. I recognised him. I think everyone recognised him. He was already quite famous and his appointment as the new director of the English Speaking Theatre had been the cause of much excitement and conversation. We might even have been talking about it just then although I do not think we knew Claude was actually there.

He walked over towards the group, our gaze acting as an invitation to him to join us. Claude was young too. I need to remember that. I always do because I never knew Claude as middle aged or older as I now am. He walked over to our group and introduced himself. He was cheerful and unaffected. He seemed surprised that we were all to some degree star struck. He asked if he could join us and someone fetched a chair. I moved my chair to one side to make room for Claude. He came and sat next to me. He introduced himself to me.

"I'm Claude," he said.

"I'm Ben," I said.

Part Three

Friederike looked at her father's face. She looked in the way Claude had taught her when she had been learning her craft. What was the mask of her father's face showing and what was it concealing? He was not an actor. Yet this trick for her of looking beyond the part being played to the heart of the person, to the character, remained the closest she came to seeing what he was really thinking. Today, now that this strange woman Alain had introduced them to had left, she detected tiredness. Perhaps it was sadness.

"I do not dislike Catherine," she said to him.

He nodded. She remained seated at the desk in Ben's old office and Herr Winter stood. He considered the meeting had gone as well as he could have expected. Meeting Catherine for the first time, he was pleased with her demeanour and genteel air of politeness. What else he might have been expecting he could not say. But this was satisfactory. His daughter had been to see Catherine's exhibition earlier in the year. She had not introduced herself at that time but had bought one of the pots Catherine was exhibiting. She liked it and it stood on one of the tables in the Grenoble house which she had now made her own home. Herr Winter preferred to spend the majority of his time here in Versur. Friederike limited her visits. Since she had become the Institute's Chief Executive, she had preferred to work from the family home in

Grenoble. She knew that she still required Herr Winter's approval. This thwarted her but was unavoidable. Most frustrating for her was the continued closure of the English Speaking Theatre. When she had stood down as its Director those years earlier to take on the Chief Executive role, it had not been possible to find a suitable replacement. The English Speaking Theatre was not the lure it had once been and it was for her too sad to run it as just another provincial theatre.

"I think she will cooperate," she added.

"Yes."

Herr Winter was impassive and Friederike wondered in some sense whether or not he really cared any longer.

"We will leave her until after the unveiling of my father's statue."

Friederike considered the statue an eccentricity on the part of her father. Many invitations had been issued and a large crowd of the best parts of society were expected. The President's office had confirmed he would be making an appearance. The weather now was fine and should be perfect for the day a week hence when the unveiling would take place at noon. The occasion provided the perfect opportunity to ensure Versur was at its best. The gardens, she felt, had become overgrown, although Herr Winter preferred a degree of naturalness bordering on wildness. She had had her way and the grounds were now restored to a greater horticultural discipline. She found the campus more like a university from the 60s, although it predated those places and perhaps had shaped their design through what had been its innovatory approach to space and materials. What she saw was a dated group of buildings that were faring badly, both actually and in taste. She felt that Versur needed reinventing yet she hesitated while her father clung on to his memories of it as a place of refinement and a legacy from Herr Winter senior.

So the statue of her grandfather was an oddity. It had been commissioned from what she considered to be a less than cutting edge sculptor and the result was a true to life figure that felt more nineteenth than twenty-first century. Herr Winter was delighted. The figure was a little less than life size, deliberately, to underplay the element of aggrandisement. If the intention had been to deflect criticism, the opposite was the most likely consequence. Friederike noted that despite the gathering promising to be a big social event, very Paris Match, there was no interest from the more serious arts media. Herr Winter had not commented on this.

It was Alain who had persuaded Catherine to share the Ben book with the Winters. He enjoyed his sporadic discussions with her through Skype and the occasional email. She sent him copies of the various documents she turned up as she worked her way through the archive. He could help her with the practical aspects of her work. Still she had refused to share any part of the manuscript with him. He was frustrated with this. Also, although he was not a man to feel any particular bitterness, he had been surprised first by the archive itself in Ben's flat and then the peculiarity of leaving everything to Catherine. Catherine by her own admission was a relative stranger. So the turn of events, Catherine writing effectively a ghosted autobiography of his former colleague, struck him as something in which he should somehow be playing a more prominent part. He could not think how exactly. When Catherine confirmed the previous December that she had completed the first draft of the book, he became very determined to read it and to that end arranged a visit to London.

Catherine was delighted to see him. It was January by the time he made it there, over a year since his last visit for the sad event of Ben's illness and all too premature death. He liked Catherine. It enabled him to be even more forgiving of Ben's decision to leave so much to her. In fact, her strange idea of trying to construct the events of Ben's life from his archive perhaps justified Ben's instinct to leave so much to her. Who else, except him, would have any interest? Naturally the family would be interested. Since Ben had been specifically forbidden to retain any records from the Winter Archive, it was better that he, Alain was not part of his posthumous arrangements.

They met first at the College in Crouch End where Catherine had a part time teaching appointment. She was keen to show him her latest work. They had coffee in a draughty canteen that was part of the college. It was mid-afternoon and there were few students about as the spring term hadn't started. Catherine introduced him to her former student and now collaborator, Kate. In her own mind, Catherine still called the pots her Ben pots, but it was Kate who had led the way in developing her own creative response to her work on Ben's book.

We have been working on a show at the end of next term she told him. He was genuinely interested to see the pots but surprised that so far Catherine had not referred to the book. She and Kate were keen to show him the first batch of pots they had been working on together for the show and he was obliged to drink his coffee quickly slightly burning the roof of his mouth.

They went to one of the studio areas where the finished pots were placed on racks. They were potted by Catherine, Kate explained, but the ideas of the pots were a collaboration between them. He carefully took them in. To be honest, they looked like over large concrete flower troughs. They were strangely rectangular yet appeared elliptical. Each was shaped uniquely. On their large blank, grey surfaces appeared odd flashes of bright colours – different glazes, Kate explained. She asked him to hold and feel one of the pots, handing it carefully to him. He felt tentative, aware that whatever his opinion these were important works for the two women he was meeting. When he held the pot, he understood, for it belied its appearance and was light as if made of polythene. The women both saw his smile. He could see they were pleased, delighted like small children playing a clever trick. He remembered the pot Catherine had given him the year before. Now he realised that was an immediate ancestor of these more beautiful pots.

He carefully replaced the pot on the shelf, now familiar with what made it inherently creative. Kate explained that the next stage of the project was to make a series of smaller pots that would work in a more domestic setting. He asked them how it was possible for the pots to look like they were made of concrete and yet weigh nothing. They again smiled and Kate went into a detailed explanation about double walled pottery. Catherine asked him what she should change. He said nothing. Each piece was unique and special. She asked him if he would like one of the pots and he was himself delighted. She had not visited his flat and asked him whether he preferred a large or smaller piece. He left the decision to her. He would definitely make it fit with his own decorations.

Catherine was pleased. She would send it to him after the show. The show was scheduled for May in the college's little gallery. Kate hoped he would be able to pop back for it.

He enjoyed their company, the pots, the unexpectedness of meeting here and not talking about the Ben book. Catherine clearly liked Kate who seemed slightly in awe of her former teacher now her collaborator. Kate preferred, he learned, to decorate rather than to pot. His suggestion to them both was maybe to allow Kate to become directly involved in the glazing and decoration of the next batch of pots. Catherine was thoughtful. When he asked if Kate had read the Ben book, Kate just laughed. It was for Catherine to tell him that the recently finished Ben book was a bone of contention between herself and Kate. It had taken up so much of her time, that the project for the new pots had been severely delayed. Although Kate added that she believed the inspiration had largely come about as a result of the year Catherine had spent in the archives, as she termed it. Alain took what they both said at face value. Kate has a copy on her computer, Catherine confirmed. No one, it appeared, had read the book.

It was Kate who had suggested the very successful Christmas dinner for Catherine's French friend the year before and Catherine was keen to repeat her earlier success. Alain agreed to visit her at the flat the following evening before he left the two women working in the studio for the rest of the day.

Catherine did send Alain the pot after the show in May. It was after he had persuaded her first to allow him to read the Ben book, and more controversially, to allow the Winters to see a copy. That in turn led to the trip to Grenoble to visit Alain and the meeting with the Winters, father and daughter.

Friederike admitted to herself that she dreaded the unveiling of the statue. However, its potential for kitsch was overshadowed by the magnificent self-importance of the event itself. Even Friederike was impressed by the elegant speech by the President of the Republic no less before he literally pulled the cord and the shroud concealing the figure fell to the floor. Given the size of the affair, it was difficult for most of the assembled guests to see the statue itself. That would need to wait for a quieter and more reflective moment. For those interested there would be plenty of opportunities to view the piece at their leisure during or after the lunchtime refreshments served immediately after the President's act of unveiling. Friederike who was especially careful about arrangements was delighted that the choice of the morning worked perfectly. It meant that the lunch could be enjoyed in the relative warmth of the day before the heat intensified and made the outdoors unpleasant by mid-afternoon.

The President left shortly after his speech. With her father she shook hands with him as he departed. He commented on how much he had learned from the late Herr Winter Senior. Herr Winter purred with appreciation and Friederike felt a strong sense of loyalty to him, to her family and to the Institute itself. Looking round at the beautifully decked out Versur – a small stand had been erected in front of the unveiling ceremony – that loyalty translated into a pride for what had been achieved here. It was her duty and job to maintain the Institute's reputation, a task her father would support and oversee her in. She sighed at that thought. It prevented her, she felt increasingly as the days went by, from making the more fundamental changes needed if the Institute were to remain culturally important for more than her generation. So the loyalty was tinged with regret and the pride marred by frustration.

Friederike did not share Herr Winter's profound concern about the book that had so oddly emerged written by their former archivist. It was Alain who had alerted them to its existence. He had been in London visiting his former boss when Ben was taken ill and died so suddenly and unexpectedly. Given the time that had passed since Ben had left Versur, no one from the family had thought it necessary to visit and flowers were discouraged. The Winters had largely forgotten about Ben's death. They would have no interest in what happened to his possessions. Ben very much belonged to the past. Herr Winter felt a slight annoyance that the young man he had hired to sort out the Hirschlich provenance had never really got to grips with the project. Friederike, because of her attachment to Claude, was always gentler and retained a fondness for him which led her to mourn his death in her own manner.

Alain had approached Friederike after returning from London and Ben's funeral. He had told her about Catherine, about the unexpected bequest to her of all his old colleague's possessions. He had also referred to some papers – photos, newspaper cuttings – that Catherine had shown him since he knew Ben and his work. Catherine, he had explained, was a relatively new and informal acquaintance. Friederike, who had met Alain at the Grenoble house, had at that stage, 18 months before the unveiling of the statue, not thought to speak to Herr Winter. She knew he would be upset if there were loose ends. He always took every opportunity to control everything that was written or said about the family and the Institute, a grip which served to maintain its reputation as an engine for cultural and educational growth. Questions were rarely asked as there was no need. She asked Alain to keep her in touch with any developments in case there was anything that might in some way relate to the Winters.

Alain had decided not to tell Friederike about the archive or even hint at the scale of the records Ben had kept at the Bloomsbury flat. He was aware of the letter of dismissal and the conditions that no items or records belonging to the Institute or family should be retained and the accompanying gagging order. Alain knew from his own experience that the Winters would take less than kindly if they realised the scale of the breach of these conditions. He did not wish to make Catherine's life more complicated than it needed to be. Then Catherine had explained to him her project for writing the Ben book. He knew that he would need, carefully, somehow, to prevent the disruption the book might possibly cause the Winters. This was not out of any loyalty. It was an instinct of preservation or recognising that for Catherine and himself there was no point in attempting to take on the Institute. It would be a fool's errand, and for Catherine a fool's errand that was not of her own making. He did wonder if this was part of a mischievousness on the part of Ben but didn't pursue the thought.

The delicious lunch at the unveiling meant that the event did not run long into the afternoon. Those who wished to see the statue had more than enough time to admire it. Most were the elderly critics and beneficiaries of the Institute who had known Herr Winter Senior as the influential elder statesmen or were the oldest and deepest friends of Herr Winter himself and understood the importance to him of honouring his father in this way. The consequence was that by 3pm the guests had left and there was a sadness about the place. Herr Winter, in the heat, had retreated to his own apartment for some rest. Friederike accompanied him there and then, with her own mixed emotions, drove back to Grenoble. There had originally been talk of a splendid dinner in the Winter's Grenoble house, but Friederike had been lukewarm, suggesting that, given the age of the majority of people likely to be invited to this more intimate family affair, it may prove all too much for a single day. She felt, driving back, that she had been right about that although Herr Winter she knew would have enjoyed the sense of occasion. The presidential address, the large number of dignitaries, how good Versur appeared and the general sense of approval for the greatness of the Herr Winter Senior the man, these were all she felt, sufficient. More than sufficient, they were tremendous. A success and she patted herself on the back, pleased now to be alone.

Alain had invited Catherine to his flat for dinner after the unveiling. They had both been on the periphery of the event. Friederike had waved at Alain, but that was the only acknowledgement and they were both too distant from the Winters themselves for any greater contact or familiarity. It was the first time Catherine had been to Alain's place. Earlier in the week they had eaten together in a restaurant, visited the museum and had a couple of coffees.

They continued to enjoy each other's company. There didn't seem any shortage of topics of conversation. Catherine was taken aback when she entered Alain's living room. The flat seemed quite large. It was in a modern block but still close to the older part of the city. In the hallway, Catherine had seen several doors suggesting a number of rooms. The living room, where Alain had directed her before offering her a drink, was large with a sliding door leading to a balcony. The balcony was sizeable enough to accommodate tables and chairs. Alain slid open the door and the warmth flooded in. He asked her if she preferred to eat inside or outside. Noting the quite loud traffic noise coming from the balcony she preferred to stay indoors for now. Later it would be quieter, so it might be pleasanter then.

One reason, she realised, the flat was so spacious was the noticeable absence of objects, even furniture. Most striking was Catherine's own pot, the one she had sent over after the show in May. Its ugliness or ungainliness, intended as its own commentary on its materiality, grated with the calm emptiness in which it was an almost unspeakable presence.

"It works, doesn't it?" he asked her.

"Maybe, maybe," she replied.

She paused. She had trusted Alain. From the beginning of these strange events, he had been the one she had relied on. She did not know why the presence of her pot would make her doubt that. She had not even thought about it before. He had been her Skype companion on the journey of understanding Ben's life. Now, for her, because of him, she understood that her pots were ugly. It was not a bad ugliness. But they were like those old master portraits of the very old, whose accuracy denied revulsion.

"I think," he said, "that the Winters both believe the Ben book is an original. I mean they believe Ben wrote it before he died and you found it amongst his papers. They don't know about the archive. They think it is a true autobiography."

Catherine was stunned.

Her extended stay was due to end immediately after her appointment with the Winters. Her flight departed early evening from Lyon airport. She did not know how long her meeting with Herr Winter and Friederike would last. They had asked her to come to the Grenoble house at 10am, two days after the unveiling. She would not have the opportunity to see Alain again in person after this dinner. She had found out from him something of what to expect.

She arrived at the house a little before ten. The weather continued to be hot and she wore a cool, sleeveless summer dress. She had checked out of the hotel and left her suitcase there to collect on her way to the airport. She planned to take the train and the hotel was conveniently between the Winter residence and the station. As her stay had been extended, she had needed to buy some more clothes including the dress she was wearing today. That was something of an extravagance from the Galeries Lafayette in the centre, although she consoled herself that it had been reduced as part of their summer collection.

A man answered the door – butler, she thought – and asked her to take a seat in the hallway. The house was much as she had imagined. The hall was austere, not grand but certain of itself with an elegantly curving staircase leading to the upper floors and an elaborate wrought iron balustrade. As she waited she also considered Alain's comments at dinner about this meeting. He had suggested that she should expect the Winters to make her some kind of offer. She probed him, not understanding. He tried to reassure her but achieved the reverse when he said she shouldn't be surprised if there was a lawyer present at some stage of the meeting. He had called it a meeting, and she guessed that it was for the Winters some kind of business event. She struggled to understand what business the Winters would wish to transact with her. "They will want the book," Alain had concluded.

Promptly at ten the butler reappeared and showed her into the front room set out with sofas and armchairs. He offered her coffee, which she accepted. The Winters waited, standing as she came into the room. The room was much more ornate than she had imagined. Wooden panels in a soft pastel with delicate scrolls of golden borders greeted her. She let out a little gasp of surprise. It was not the room on the first floor she had described from Ben's first visit there. How could they believe Ben's book was other than a fake, a fiction?

"Louis Seize," explained Friederike. "One of the family had the whole room shipped from an eighteenth-century French chateau."

The ornate panelling was matched by the embroidered furniture and period tables and a desk. She was now taken aback to see one of her pots, so taken aback she actually veered off her course of greeting Herr Winter with his outstretched hand, to check that it was in fact one of hers. It was one from the show, a large version of the double walled, minimally glazed pots.

"We love, well I love, your pots. I came over to your show. Alain suggested I should."

The momentary doubt about Alain and how much he had told them and why resurfaced in Catherine's mind. If Catherine had been more composed, she would have asked Friederike why she had not introduced herself at the show. Instead she veered back towards Herr Winter and shook his hand. Friederike kissed her on both cheeks. Feeling slightly man handled and a bit off balance, Catherine made it to the seat where she assumed she was to sit and the butler handed her the cup of coffee.

Herr Winter smiled. "I do also like the pot," he said tilting his head towards his daughter. "I am just not sure whether it works best in this room. This is a favourite room of mine. It has been since I was a child."

Friederike gave the answer to Catherine's unasked question. She was sorry to have missed Catherine at her exhibition. She had had to fit it in around other engagements in the UK and Catherine had not been at the gallery when she had visited. She knew in any case that they would be meeting later in the year to discuss the book Ben had written. Catherine thought about this. She knew the pot had been sold very early in the run of the show. She thought at the opening. Certainly it was one of the larger items and she remembered how excited she had been at the sale which encouraged other purchases and helped to ensure the success of the exhibition.

"In fact," Friederike went on, "I was able to meet the owner of the gallery and to discuss a potential sponsorship by the Winter Institute to support your work and a future, larger exhibition. Everyone at the Winter Institute would be so excited to work with you—"

"That is correct," Herr Winter intervened. "Before speaking about that aspect of our arrangements, it is necessary to speak about the book you received as part of the legacy from Ben. I believe you only knew Ben quite recently. It must have been a surprise when you received such a legacy. We were so glad you have been speaking to Alain about it, as he has been able to let us know what is happening."

Catherine wanted to reply but Herr Winter held up his hand to stop her and he continued speaking.

"I think, if you do not mind, that we would all benefit if we had our lawyer present."

Alain had been right about that too.

"We do not wish to cause you any undue anxiety. It is just that in our experience, having an objective legal record of what we are agreeing is helpful. In case we have different recollections of that agreement."

Now Catherine was responding as she had to the odd conversation with Alain the previous evening. The terms that were used. What agreement was Herr Winter talking about?

"Is it acceptable about the lawyer?"

Catherine nodded. Herr Winter made a small gesture to the butler who had remained in the room and the lawyer was summoned. There were brief introductions, then the lawyer sat at the ornate desk. He had suggested to Catherine that she pretend he was not there. He would simply take notes.

"What agreement?" Catherine said.

"We shall, of course come to that. First, the book. Ben speaks plainly about his illegal accumulation of Winter Institute papers at his London flat. The flat he left you in his will. These must be returned to us here. We would not expect you to bear the cost of this. We will organise their collection at a convenient time.

"Next, and most painful, is the tissue of lies Ben has woven around the provenance of the Hirschlich collection. I cannot imagine what caused a valued and trusted former employee of the Institute to insinuate these horrible untruths. Not only a valued and trusted employee, but one who worked closely, very closely with me over many years. Someone who was also trusted by my daughter whom I encouraged to return that trust and value his opinion. There is and can be no questions raised over the way in which the Hirschlich collection came into the ownership of the Winter Institute. It is vile and inhuman to treat the memory of a Holocaust victim such as Herr Hirschlich with such disrespect. In fact, I would contrast this vileness with the generosity and humanity with which the Winter Institute has honoured the memory of Herr Hirschlich by making his art collection available to the public and honouring him as the great collector and dealer he was and would have continued to be if he had not been murdered.

"It is not acceptable that these lies – lies that you have almost accidentally been caught up in – should exist at all. That is why the Winter Institute will also require all copies, physical and electronic, of this vile book to be handed over. That is part of the agreement. We have already secured Alain's copy. Any evidence that this condition has been breached will lead to immediate recovery of any sums paid as part of the agreement.

"On a much more pleasant note, my daughter touched on how much the Institute appreciates your fine ceramic work. It is original, creative and, we believe, of international artistic importance. For that reason, we would wish to offer you a five year sponsored residency with the Winter Institute. In addition to the generous stipend, there would also be opportunities for visits and demonstrations. I see you look taken aback. Let me assure you that by residency, we do not mean you live here. We imagine you would prefer to live where you do now. We would, as I say be keen for you to offer demonstrations at Versur and arrange other visits. We have an excellent staff to make the appropriate links. The Winter name, I say it myself, has cachet in the cultural world others find hard to match. And let me remind you, you retain

Ben's London flat. That is itself for you an unexpected and significant benefit of your short acquaintance with him."

He stopped speaking. Catherine finally understood that the lawyer did actually have this agreement already. There did not seem an opportunity for questions. That did not appear to come as part of the way this worked.

"What about Willi?" she asked. She asked them both, looking from one to the other.

"You see" – Herr Winter sounded irritated if not angry – "that is the danger of a book that is simply a pack of lies. What Willi? Does he ring true to you? These are fictions. So much of the book Ben has written is a fiction. Remember, Friederike and I were both there. So much of it seems made up, and to what purpose, to damage the name of the Winter Institute. We know, once these rumours appear people believe them. Even though I know that the Winter family has made such an enormous contribution to, yes, to humanity, especially through the Winter Institute, there are still some, a small number, who resent us and who wish to damage us. That cannot be allowed to happen. That is why we know you will realise, especially as a direct beneficiary of our purpose of culture and education, how important it is that these lies never see the light of day."

Catherine looked around the room. Distracted, each time her eyes found her own pot; she still admired its intense elegance. Like Versur, perhaps the room was somehow similar, if on a different floor, to her description in the book, but at the same time completely different, separate. So too the words from Herr Winter reminded her of what she had written when Ben had been removed from his post. Yet to hear them first hand was a completely different experience. The effect, which she had not realised, was to sledgehammer her into compliance. How, she wondered, as she continued to look around the room for answers, could it be an agreement when she had never agreed. The room answered back. She would agree.

"This is how it must be," she heard Herr Winter say. There was a silence. She did not know whether she was expected to speak. She was looking at a single pilaster gilded candlestick about the height of an eight year old that stood between the double windows. It was, she concluded, quite unpleasant, gross even. It was just an object. The room left her in no doubt that she would soon be sitting down with the lawyer to confirm her agreement to the agreement. That was it, the agreement was something separate from her will. It was her port of entry, her admission to the Winter Institute. Now she would be a full member with all the perks and privileges. She would be obliged to abide by the rules when she had never even asked to join or knew what she was getting into.

It was Friederike's turn to speak.

"We are delighted, we will be delighted, that you are becoming a fellow of the Winter Institute. There are only a small number of people each year whom we select as fellows. The support is extensive. You will see it is set out in the agreement. I hope that you will take up our offer for the first exhibition of your work at Versur to coincide with next summer's festival at the English Speaking Theatre."

"Yes, it is true," Friederike responded to Catherine who had turned her gaze from her exploration of the room to look with surprise at her. "It is wonderful. We are to reopen the theatre. I think this is the triumph of my initial years in the role of Director of the Winter Institute. Of course, you know that I was myself the director there for a number of years. Then, for a time, the theatre lost its way. I think we can be honest about that. I think the theatre did not maintain its links with the vibrant contemporary theatre world. People, audiences, that had loved its work grew older, like my dear father, and we failed to attract a younger audience with up to date works.

"Well, the plan is coming to fruition and we will focus our work on LGBTQ work. It is my personal homage to Claude. Claude is my still-missed wonderful mentor and this will mean his memory is rightly honoured in a genuinely contemporary manner. One more thing, but this is strictly confidential and not to be shared, please, as we want to make a splash with it, we shall be renaming the theatre. It is, crudely put, a rebranding, but I know it is profoundly more than that and part of making this of our own age. We shall be calling the theatre the *Claude Berners Theatre*. We wish to keep its international European identity and our shared sense of heritage, the heritage of the Winter Institute across Europe."

She paused. Catherine nodded as if applauding. Friederike continued.

"So it will be a great honour for us, and I hope for you, to see your pots exhibited in the refurbished theatre foyers during the festival."

More nodding. So that was assent of a kind. Catherine knew she was assenting to everything the two Winters presented her with. She assented to the agreement whether or not she agreed with it. That, on receiving so much from the Winters, was as far as she could go in assimilating what had just happened.

"What would you like me to do?" she asked.

"Well, rather straightforwardly," Herr Winter replied, "to agree."

So that is what I did she explained to Alain in their unexpected dinner the same evening after describing her encounter of the morning.

The rest of the day had not gone to plan. She spent at least an hour with the lawyer after the Winters had graciously excused themselves. She spoke hardly at all. He explained everything, insisted that she read the five page document. She tried to flick through it, but he was sat beside her and made clear he needed her to have read every word or he might as well have read it to her out loud. It was comprehensive as far as she could tell. No angle of her commitments was omitted alongside severe penalties if she breached these conditions. She had no idea of its legal status. The butler was fetched when it came time to witness her signature. Herr Winter had already signed on behalf of the Winter Institute.

Staggering out of the house she collected her suitcase from the hotel on the way to the station and took the train to Lyon Airport to discover that her flight had been cancelled. She even momentarily thought it was a plot by the Winters so that they could delay her and make sure they got all the papers out of Ben's flat in case she tried to hide some. Then she realised that was absurd. The Winters worked through the law. Now they had the agreement, they would always be ahead however she acted. They had the advantage she had surrendered.

The airline sent her a text with details of a Lyon hotel where they had booked her a room. She would have to rebook her flight herself and that was it. She got a taxi to the hotel. It was modern, on the outskirts of the city near the motorway.

There was a flight with availability the following day so she managed to book herself on to this. Another day here. It felt like she was not allowed to get away. She was worn out with stretching her limited luggage day after day. The hotel was surprisingly helpful with an overnight laundry service and that did cheer her up.

She rang Alain. It was an impulsive action. She was not sure how much she trusted Alain now. He had been in league with the Winters, but only up to a point. She did not know if he had been sent to spy on her. His mission in visiting Ben and then attending the funeral might have been to be the representative of the Winters, ensuring their interests were best served. Still he was Ben's friend. She believed that from what both he and Ben had said to her. He had not revealed to the Winters their mistake in believing the book was actually authored by Ben. He had not told them about the archive which he had only known about after the funeral when he came to dinner with her at the Bloomsbury flat. They had only learned about the archive from the Ben book itself. This reassured her. Still there was something for her sinister about his continuing to know the Winters, his friendship with Friederike. How different was that from how she was now drawn into their net she didn't like to think.

Alain picked up. From his voice she could tell he was pleased to hear from her. He would be curious about how the morning with the Winters had gone. Now it was early evening he imagined she would be calling from London. She explained what had happened. He was sorry she hadn't rung sooner as he could have come and collected her from the airport himself and she could have stayed the night at his flat. She didn't attempt to explain why she hadn't done this. It had actually never occurred to her, although when he said it this would have been an obvious plan. She realised that calling him impulsively she did not really know why.

Alain was keen to know about the meeting. Catherine explained this was too difficult to explain over the phone. He understood. He suggested driving over to the hotel for a late dinner. She hesitated, said it was too late and too far, then agreed so now they were seated in the hotel dining room, the only people there and the restaurant now closed for further orders.

Alain was not surprised she had signed. "Everyone always does." The way the Winters worked was well known to him. "It's how all of these people operate."

She valued the debrief, then felt the extreme of fatigue the day demanded. She was too tired to continue the conversation. She wished to excuse herself. She needed to be ready for her flight the following afternoon. Yet Alain insisted on a moment or too longer. He understood that she was exhausted. Of course, it had been a monumental day for her, but also, he said, for him. He needed, why now, why here, he did not know, but he needed to tell her the importance he attached to her work of the last year and a half. She was Ben's true biographer. As a stranger, she could see things that he as a colleague and then close friend could not see. He felt her book was really important.

"Did they actually say Willi never existed?" he asked.

"I don't think so. It is very hard to remember. I don't think they said it in so many words."

"It was implied?"

"Strongly implied, very strongly."

"But they could deny that they had said he never existed?"

"Yes. Anyway, what does it matter. There was no one else to say otherwise. They could simply have lied. My word would never matter against theirs." She thought about the two photos with Willi in them.

"They don't lie. They are too smart for that. I know Willi exists. I never met him, but Ben spoke about him. Who knows where he is now, but if the book came out someone would track him down."

"Why would anyone bother?" she asked, so tired she found it hard to imagine why anyone would.

"Why did you bother to write the book?" he countered.

Alain told her he believed in the conclusions she had reached in the book. He absolutely believed that these were the conclusions Ben had himself come to when he sought her friendship and decided to leave her his archive, all his possessions. She laughed at that and told him how the Winters had congratulated her on her inheritance, almost as if the Bloomsbury flat had been a gift from them. Then she understood, as Alain did, with no need to speak, that in so many ways it was.

"There are groups who would bother," Alain said. "I have made my own enquiries. Organisations like the *German Lost Art Foundation*. Groups like that. Those are the ones the Winters fear. Think about it."

He spoke some more about why he wanted her to do this. Catherine felt too tired to think or listen. They left the empty restaurant. She did feel reassured. It had been OK to trust Alain. Now it really was time to get back to London. In London she could speak about it all to Kate.

She had not visited the Bloomsbury flat since her return from Grenoble. She felt barred from it. She felt as if she had committed the crime. She waited in her home. The company organising the shipment of the Ben archive back to Versur were in touch immediately. They sent a courier to fetch a key for the flat. Luckily she had a spare. Even so she felt she had handed over the keys to her kingdom. She continued to wait even after the courier had gone with the spare key. She wanted to lie down. Instead, she decided to go to the studio at the college. There she would seek out Kate. Kate whom she needed to speak to about all of this. Kate who, unlike Alain who was too involved himself, could help her understand what was happening. Happening to her and happening to her and the Winters and everyone. How, she still queried with this dull tiredness, had all this come about.

Kate was not at the college. Catherine saw her finished pots on the racks in the studio where she and Kate worked. Her success in the show earlier in the year had been rewarded by additional hours of teaching and extra space for her work. Now all this work was owned by the Winters and she had started to work for them. That is how it felt to her. That was the agreement.

She rang Kate. Kate was at home. Catherine had never visited Kate at home. She had never thought about Kate's home, her life there. It had always been about the pots. Kate wanted to see Catherine. She wanted to hear how it had gone in Versur. So Catherine went to see her at her home.

Kate lived in a terraced house not all that far from Catherine's own flat in Crouch End. It was bigger than she had expected. She had imagined Kate's life as more or less resembling her own. It didn't. First there was a dog, a largish dog. Then, she realised, there was a family, a husband, children. Evidence of their existence spread across the hall and into the kitchen where she was now sitting speaking with Kate. She had to tell Kate in any case because she would need the electronic copy of the Ben book she had given her returned. When she got to that part of what had happened, Kate simply said no. Catherine didn't understand. Kate looked angry. Angry with Catherine who didn't understand why. Kate explained. There was no agreement. Who cares what Catherine had signed. It didn't matter. She did not need to abide by a single part of what she had committed to in the agreement.

Catherine talked about the law, about the lawyer. Sure, Kate grimaced, but what the Winters didn't know they couldn't stop. Catherine should hold on to the key parts of the archive, the critical documents that had led her to write a book so credible that the Winters actually thought Ben had written it himself. That was tell-tale in itself. It would be an act of desecration not to keep the book and the evidence. Desecration, Kate explained, to what she thought of as a work of art. It was a creative act and the Winters, agreement or not, could not be allowed to destroy it.

Catherine simply was not able, before speaking with Kate, to see this as an option. She had taken the agreement exactly as it was written. That is why she felt in thrall to the Winters. But it was too late. She told Kate about the courier and the spare key. Kate was equally adamant. They must do their best to recover the items from the flat. It would take time to organise the emptying of the flat. They would need vans. They would need permission from the Council to park their vans while they were loading them up. They had certainly got hold of the key as quickly as possible, but if they went to Bloomsbury now, there was a good chance they could recover what was needed. Catherine was impressed with Kate's practical knowledge. She put it down to having a family and a dog.

Kate led the way as Catherine double checked she had the key to the flat with her. They decided to take the bus. Turning into the road with the nearest bus stop, they saw a 91 just leaving. Another twenty minute wait at the bus stop. Another opportunity for Kate to speak about how Catherine owed the Winters nothing. She had every right to keep back what she wanted and did not have to hand over every copy of her book. She was only doing the same as Ben. It wouldn't matter. They would never find out.

As they stood waiting for the bus, not knowing if they would be in time to salvage what was needed from the flat, Catherine told Kate about her last conversation with Alain. That Alain thought they should both consider contacting some groups about lost and stolen art. His idea was that Hirschlich the art dealer was simply a cover for holding on to art that been stolen from numerous sources but no one was looking for because its provenance was too obscure or there were no survivors from the original owners and families. Perhaps there had been the core of a collection stolen from a single individual, even a dealer. Perhaps that had given the Winters the idea of assembling such a collection of stolen works. They would have had plenty of contacts in Germany during the war and living in Switzerland made the thefts easy and practical.

The conversation was interrupted by the arrival of the bus. They stopped talking about the Winters on the bus. It was too public. That told them something about what they were dealing with. It would take over an hour, Catherine knew, to reach the flat. Normally she enjoyed the slow winding of the bus. It gave her time to think. Often she would be thinking about the book she wrote for Ben as she sat on the bus heading towards the flat. Now it felt frustratingly over long. She should have shelled out for a taxi. What if Kate was wrong. They might arrive and the flat would already be empty, everything gone, how she imagined it in her mind ever since she signed the agreement. Or they might arrive and the removers would be packing things up. Could they pretend that they had come to collect something or would the packers have been briefed that nothing should be allowed to be taken away? Catherine even imagined Friederike there supervising the whole removal and storage in person.

They were making progress, under the railway line and then past the prison. Towards the bottom of the Caledonian Road, the bus stopped. They had run into traffic as they made their way through King's Cross. It was getting hot in the summer sunshine on the bus. The bus driver opened the bus doors saying something about a burst water main and we might be stuck for a while. The two women got off the bus. They needed to walk and at least do their best to get there before it was too late. Catherine realised Kate had been thinking along the same lines.

Walking was hot as well. Catherine was wearing the wrong clothes. She had shed the summer dress she had from Grenoble and automatically assumed that London would be cooler. It was but not by much and her long sleeved shirt made out of some sportswear material made her sweat as they walked in a hurry through King's Cross. They had to stop at the pelican crossing outside the British Library and wait for the lights to change even though the traffic was at a standstill.

It felt too dangerous to pick their way through the traffic and motorcycles and bikes.

So when they eventually arrived, Catherine was too hot and Kate was breathless. She imagined what they looked like as she let herself into the main entrance of the red brick mansion block. There were no vans parked outside, so either they were in time or the flat would be empty. They were in time. She poured herself and Kate a glass of water from the bottle she kept in the fridge. Just like the first time she had arrived in the flat, she felt like a thief and in reality this time it was her intention to remove the objects around which she had constructed Ben's story.

Kate loved the flat. Catherine in all the rush to get here had forgotten this was the first time Kate had seen it. Kate found it secretive and special. She described it to Catherine as a safe house from some spy thriller. She adored the neatly organised density of records.

Catherine felt anxious. She still imagined being caught here red handed. By whom? Did she really think Friederike was about to step through the door? Or that the lawyer would politely inform her that he was calling the police. That was ridiculous. Nonetheless, she was keen to collect what she needed and then leave the rest to the Winter's removers. She knew where things were. The items she wanted she had kept out of the archive in the drawer of the desk where she had written Ben's book. The photo of Willi in Berlin. Of course Willi existed. The photo in Trieste meeting the man who claimed Hirschlich had stayed with his family fleeing the Nazis and on the way to Zagreb. She had the document from the Leipzig archive with the only record of Hirschlich's family home there. She had the photo of the much younger

Friederike in Venice, and the programme, photos and reviews from the derided production of Eugene Onegin Claude had directed while he and Ben had been living right here in this flat. The invitation to the reception honouring the Winter Institute's sponsorship of the production. Now she too was a Winter Institute sponsored artist.

Kate was keen to look through the documents. She knew them from Catherine's descriptions and because they existed she knew that what she had been told was in some way true. She told Catherine that this was really important, agreement or not. Catherine wanted to leave now. She didn't want to be caught. She was glad that she had talked to Kate and had come back for the evidence. Alain would be pleased although she didn't think she would tell him. She didn't know what would happen next. They left the flat and were in time for some oysters at the oyster bar in King's Cross station. Catherine treated Kate while she thought what she might do next.

It was over the oysters that she decided on the patio for her garden.

Kate stood with Catherine in Catherine's back garden looking at the trench that had been dug. Kate called it a hole. It was two foot in depth and square, so not really a trench thought Catherine. Still trench was the official term. Although square, it appeared diamond as the corners pointed at the front and back, left and right of the rectangular garden. The garden itself had been turned into a building site. Catherine had taken the opportunity to have electricity and water connected to the studio at the far end which also now had its own kiln. The Winter Institute stipend was proving useful. They held mugs of coffee. The late September weather was colder than it seemed. Catherine wore an overcoat. Kate was feeling the chill in her hoody and jeans. She had not expected it all to be quite so outdoors. She had not really known what to expect when Catherine asked her to come over. She had been helping Catherine over the previous three weeks by driving all her pots from the college to Catherine's home and had watched as the workmen used the little digger to create the hole in Catherine's garden. She was bemused why Catherine wanted a patio in her garden at all. She avoided asking her too many questions. For example, whether the pots – the beautifully double sided illusory concrete styled pots – were somehow to decorate the patio. An installation piece, she wondered. Perhaps to be transported to the proposed exhibition of Catherine's work in Versur the following summer.

Catherine had not spoken of the Winters very much since their dash to recover Ben's evidence. She did tell her that in the intervening two months, she had not disclosed what they had done in her calls with Alain. He was keen to visit again nearer Christmas Catherine was unsure that this ritual memorial of Ben's death was appropriate, she meant, was what she wanted.

The Winters had indeed emptied Ben's flat of all remaining traces of his archive. Catherine imagined these now safely secured in some Winter vault. Perhaps they were not even in Versur but some Swiss bank. She blamed Alain in part for her new found suspicions of the Winters who had been only munificent towards her. Buying her, maybe, but she appreciated the money and had long since abandoned any thought that she would return to Versur to exhibit. She knew she had been holding things close to her own chest, about the patio, her pots, Ben's evidence. It was because she still wasn't completely sure that she wanted to go through with the patio plan. By not telling Kate what she planned, she left herself the option of doing something different. It also meant that Kate would have very limited opportunity to dissuade her. It was true that burying the pots was unfair. They were a joint creative achievement. Kate would object on the straightforward grounds that, as well as being jointly created, it was destructive of such beautiful objects. They deserved a better fate.

Yet, Catherine, having this argument in her mind in advance with Kate rehearsed her sense that by burying the pots they were not destroying them but returning them to the earth. It was not an act of destruction but preservation. Destruction would be to smash them. If she were to seize one of the workman's spades and smash each and every one of the crude yet wonderfully delicate pots her hands had made, that would be destruction. She wanted the opposite. A permanent home where they could not be bought by the likes of the Winters. Where she supposed she could not be bought as she had been, but, she knew would never exhibit.

Once the flat was emptied, Catherine had arranged for it to be professionally decorated and let through a property management company. The company, which for a substantial proportion of the rent, took on all the upkeep of the flat, told her it was currently occupied by a charming Spanish banker who worked in the City. Even after the company had taken their cut, Catherine continued to receive a regular and sufficient income for her needs. She was planning a winter in her now heated studio. Starting again, on her own. She would spend the next six months creating her next collection.

She had wondered how the Winters would respond when she failed to show her work at Versur. Quickly, without even needing Alain to explain this time, she worked out that they were not interested. They did not contact her. The generous payment in the agreement simply appeared each month in her bank account. She knew it would do so for the next five years, because that was the agreement and as far as the Winters knew she had kept her side of the bargain. There would be no attempt from the Winters to contact her. Of course, if she had followed up with them, they would have been charming. A bright graduate trainee would have been provided to curate her exhibition and a number of internationally acclaimed potters would have been invoked to endorse any exhibition. Equally, silence meant that the agreement was honoured and she need never see them again.

She thought about Alain. She did trust him. Still, he was too close, literally in Grenoble, to the Winters to the Winter Institute to be completely relied upon. He was really the useful go between, so she continued to be thoughtful about the pricks of conscience he had revealed at the hotel just before her departure just a few months ago from Lyon, from Versur, from the unveiling of the statue of Herr Winter senior and the speech by the French President. Her plan was to lock herself away in her garden shed and make pots.

They finished their mugs of coffee and Catherine took them back into the kitchen. When she returned, she told Kate what they were now going to do. It surprised Catherine that Kate raised no objection. She intuited everything that Catherine had thought she would need to say to defend her actions. Kate went to fetch one of the larger pots and brought it over to the hole. She suggested that it might make sense to line up the pots beside the hole and then for her to hand them to Catherine who could stand in the trench and arrange them as she chose. It was a good plan. What they realised as they worked was that if they were to cover them with a layer of earth they would need to do this as they went along as otherwise they would have to stand on the pots in the trench and break them to reach those in the middle.

It was satisfying manual work. It felt quite like potting did. You needed to use your hands. It was physical. As they proceeded, Catherine took off her overcoat and hung it from the little digger. They filled the diamond shaped trench from one of its corners. Some of the larger posts were too tall to stand in the two foot depth, so Catherine laid these on their sides. They used a wheelbarrow and two spades to cover the pots with earth row by row, each row becoming longer as they worked from one corner of the diamond to another. When they had covered some rows of pots with the soil heaped to the side of the hole where the workers had left it, Catherine carefully walked across it, using her feet to compound the earth and ensure it was compacted around the artefacts. Kate looked anxious, but the pots were strong. Catherine knew they were strong. It was another contradictory feature of the double sided potting technique she had used. There were enough pots to fill three quarters of the trench.

The builders, Catherine explained, had told her they would need six inches or so to fill with sand to bed in the patio stones. It looked about right to both of them. The builders hadn't shown much interest in why Catherine wanted a deeper trench.

"Not deep enough to bury your husband," one had joked half-heartedly.

If Catherine wanted to fill the trench herself, it made no difference to them. Their expertise was in making a perfect patio where the rain water would drain off.

"I want you to pot a bird bath for the centre of the patio when it is finished," Catherine said to Kate.

Kate nodded. She would enjoy that as a project. She would come back next spring with the finished bird bath and when it was warm enough they could sit out in the garden and have a drink together and share notes on their progress in creating their next collections. Perhaps they could fix a shared exhibition at the college.

Catherine went back into the kitchen and fetched the plastic container she had left there. It had a tight fitting lid and inside the evidence was placed in a diver's water proof pouch that the internet assured her was impermeable at significant depths. She paused for a moment, looking back through the kitchen window at the partially filled trench. The work for the patio was almost completed. It would have a firm foundation. She thought again how odd that Ben's authorship was credible with people who had known him, people who had been there. She had been disappointed by the difference between the people and the places, when she had reached them, and the fictional recreation of them she had made on behalf of Ben. Reality fell short. Not that she had been everywhere or met everyone. Willi she hoped was as she had portrayed him. Claude, she was glad she had not met Claude. No one can live up to the memory of a loved one. That was not possible. Hirschlich no one had met. She thought of him hiding in the Trieste pension. Travelling on to Zagreb. One way or another he could no longer exist anymore. His collection of paintings was, she mused, stealing the show. She took the evidence outside.

"Plastic is indestructible, so they say, so that's something," she said to Kate as she placed the pouch with its photos and documents and guides in the empty corner of the trench.

What she meant, she supposed, was that the evidence was indestructible; as indestructible as the truth. Then there was so much evidence and so much truth to be had. It only counted if you knew where to look and what you were looking for.

Watched by Kate, Catherine filled in the rest of the trench, tamping down the earth with her feet. She had thought to keep one piece of evidence above ground but when she had gone through the items, she realised there was nothing of Ben, no photo, no record. So she left it all where it was in the plastic box in the trench with a copy of Ben's book in case someone one day needed a guide to what they were looking at. It was time to lay Ben to rest. It was time to lay them all to rest: Ben, Willi, Claude, the Winters, Hirschlich.

CPSIA information can be obtained
at www.ICGtesting.com
Printed in the USA
LVHW081515050521
686572LV00020B/869